Young Adult Migration: 2007–2009 to 2010–2012

American Community Survey Reports

By Megan J. Benetsky; Charlynn A. Burd, Ph.D.;
and Melanie A. Rapino, Ph.D.
March 2015
ACS-31

INTRODUCTION

Young adults in the United States have the highest rate of migration compared with other age groups. The most common reasons for moving among all ages are job, housing, or family related.[1] Many of these moves are made between the ages of 18 to 34, an age group marked by various life course transitions associated with moving.[2] These include getting a job, going to college, getting married, or having children.

YOUNG ADULTS, DEFINED

Young adults are defined as being between the ages of 18 and 34, roughly born in the late 1970s through the 1990s. They are characterized as having grown up with the Internet, and they came of age during the Great Recession.

Generally, when economic conditions are good, the rate of migration is relatively stable, regardless of age.[3] However, spurred by a credit and housing crisis, the Great Recession, which lasted from about 2007–2009, was followed by a large increase in unemployment in the United States. Accordingly, migration in the United States slowed.[4,5] Young adults may have foregone many of the life course transitions associated with moving because of fewer employment opportunities, delayed family formation, or the inability to buy a home.

This report describes the demographic and socioeconomic status of young adult migrants, aged 18 to 34 using the 2007–2009 and 2010–2012 American Community Survey (ACS) 3-year estimates. Migrants in this report include any young adults whose current address was different from their address 1 year ago. These estimates represent the years of the postrecession period using the 2010–2012 ACS 3-year estimates and were compared with the 2007–2009 ACS 3-year estimates, which represented the years of the recession period. The geographic location of young adults was also analyzed for the two time periods with a focus on metropolitan areas.

The ACS is a nationally representative, ongoing survey that produces annual estimates of socioeconomic, demographic, and housing characteristics at the national and subnational levels. The ACS 3-year estimates are a multiyear dataset collected over a 36-month period that allow a more detailed analysis of smaller populations across smaller areas of geography. The U.S. Census Bureau recommends the comparison of multiyear estimates only when the data years are not overlapping, such as the 2007–2009 and 2010–2012 datasets.[6] In the ACS, respondents were asked where they lived 1 year ago, which provided the previous residence

[1] David K. Ihrke, Carol S. Faber, and William K. Koerber, "Geographical Mobility: 2008 to 2009," *Current Population Reports*, P20-565, U.S. Census Bureau, Washington DC, 2011.

[2] Rachel S. Franklin, "Migration of the Young, Single, and College Educated: 1995 to 2000," *Census 2000 Special Reports*, CENSR-12, U.S. Census Bureau, Washington, DC, 2003; and Justyna Gowrowkowska and Todd K. Gardner, "Historical Migration of the Young, Single, and College Educated: 1965 to 2000," Population Division Working Paper No. 94, U.S. Census Bureau, Washington, DC, 2012.

[3] David K. Ihrke, Carol S. Faber, and William K. Koerber, "Geographical Mobility: 2008 to 2009, *Current Population Reports*, P20-565, U.S. Census Bureau, Washington DC, 2011.

[4] The Great Recession officially began in December of 2007 and ended in June of 2009, according to the National Bureau of Economic Research. See <www.nber.org/cycles.html>.

[5] William H. Frey, *The Great American Migration Slowdown: Regional and Metropolitan Dimensions*, Brookings, Washington, DC, 2009; and David K. Ihrke, Carol S. Faber, and William K. Koerber, "Geographical Mobility: 2008 to 2009," *Current Population Reports*, P20-565, U.S. Census Bureau, Washington DC, 2011.

[6] See <www.census.gov/acs/www/guidance_for_data_users/comparing_data/>.

U.S. Department of Commerce
Economics and Statistics Administration
U.S. CENSUS BUREAU
census.gov

(origin) information. The "residence 1 year ago" question was interpreted as a move in the last year despite the use of the 3-year datasets, rather than a move 3 years ago.[7] The current residence information was obtained from the mailing address and the previous residence was self-reported. Age was reported at the time the survey was conducted.[8]

This report is organized as follows: first, there is an overview of

[7] For more information on how to interpret ACS multiyear data, see Section 11.11 at <www.census.gov/acs/www/Downloads /survey_methodology/acs_design _methodology_ch11_2014Chapter_11 _RevisedDec2010.pdf>.

[8] All data include Puerto Rico, unless otherwise noted.

migration trends across age groups, then each time period is examined— postrecession (2010–2012) and recession (2007–2009). For each time period, we examine the mobility trends for young migrants as well as their demographic and socioeconomic characteristics. Finally, there is an analysis of the geography of young inmovers by metropolitan areas.

HIGHLIGHTS

- Young adults had higher migration rates than the total population.

- The number of young adults who moved between the 2007–2009 recession period and the 2010–2012 postrecession period declined by about half of a million people.

- The migration rate of young adults declined about 1.4 percentage points from the 2007–2009 recession period to the 2010–2012 postrecession period.

- Young adults aged 18 to 24 had the highest migration rate compared to 25- to 29-year-olds and 30- to 34-year-olds in both the 2007–2009 recession period and the 2010–2012 postrecession period, and also had the largest decline from the 2007–2009 recession period to the 2010–2012 postrecession period.

- Young adult females aged 18 to 24 had a higher migration rate than young adult men 18 to 24 in the 2010–2012 postrecession period, while young adult males overall had larger declines between periods compared with women.

- Native-born young adults had larger declines between periods than the foreign born.

- Young adults with a college degree had the smallest declines in migration compared to young adults with less education.

- Many smaller metros, especially ones with colleges, had larger shares of young adult inmovers than large metro areas.

YOUNG ADULTS ARE THE MOST MOBILE POPULATION

Migration in the United States is largely driven by young adults and the children that accompany them. The migration rate declines after young adulthood as more people have completed the markers of adulthood transitions like completing education, getting a job, getting married, and buying a home. These life events connected to transitions to adulthood tend to be associated with moving as well. Using the 2007–2009 and 2010–2012 ACS 3-year estimates, Figure 2 shows this trend across age. Children aged 1 to 6 had migration rates higher than that of the total population. This was because children typically move with their parents, many of whom are young adults. The migration rate went up at age 18, peaked at about age 23, and continued to stay above the total population average until the late 30s.

Figure 2 also shows that migration rates in the 2010–2012 postrecession period tracked closely to migration rates in the 2007–2009 recession period, except across the young adult ages. From age 18 to 30 there was a significant decline in migration in the 2010–2012 postrecession period compared with the 2007–2009 recession period due to about a half-million fewer young adult movers between these periods.

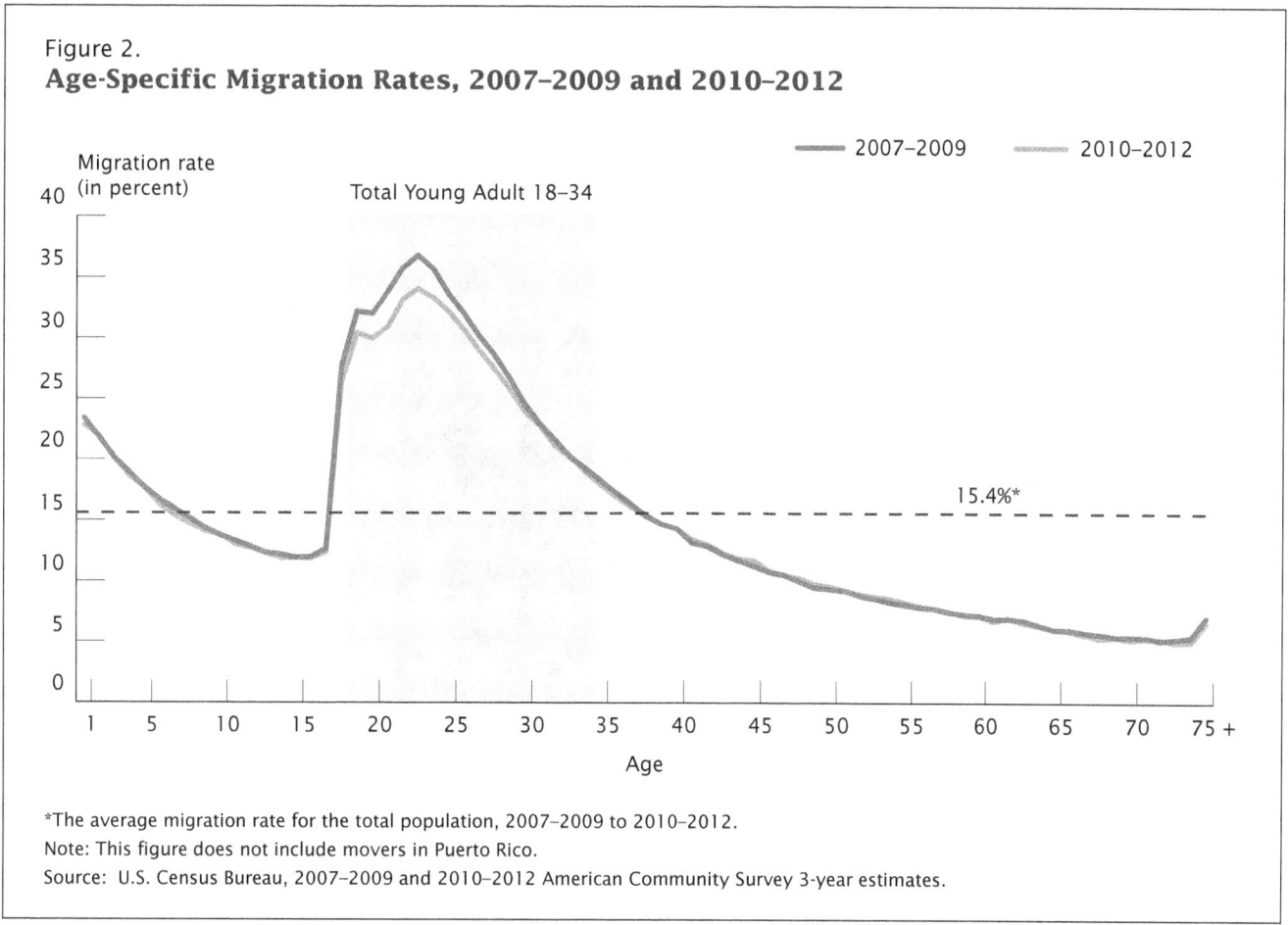

Figure 2.
Age-Specific Migration Rates, 2007–2009 and 2010–2012

━━━ 2007–2009   ━━━ 2010–2012

Migration rate (in percent)

Total Young Adult 18–34

15.4%*

Age

*The average migration rate for the total population, 2007–2009 to 2010–2012.
Note: This figure does not include movers in Puerto Rico.
Source: U.S. Census Bureau, 2007–2009 and 2010–2012 American Community Survey 3-year estimates.

While most young adults experience major life course transitions, there is a relatively large range in age (17 years) in the 18- to 34-year-old sample, which may mask variations in the likelihood to migrate or the location of migration. For example, 18- to 24-year-olds are more likely to move to areas with universities, while 25- to 29-year-olds' migration patterns may be job-driven, and 30- to 34-year-olds may seek out areas with affordable housing for a family in addition to employment opportunities. For this reason, this analysis separates young adults into three groups: 18- to 24-year-olds, 25- to 29-year-olds, and 30- to 34-year-olds. This helps to capture differences between those who are

still enrolled in school or who are not in school and those who have likely completed their education.

Figure 3 shows the age distribution for the total population and for movers. Young Adults made up about 23.7 percent of the total population of the United States, while they accounted for over 43 percent of all movers. About 20.8 percent of all movers were between the ages of 18 and 24, accounting for almost half of all young adult movers. This is followed by 13.2 percent of all movers aged 25 to 29 and about 9.5 percent between 30 and 34 years. The 18- to 24-year-old age grouping is larger than the 25- to 29-year-old group and those aged 30 to 34, due to a 7-year age range

rather than a 5-year range. However, young adults aged 18 to 24 were grouped together because, in many tables and reports by the Census Bureau, educational attainment is usually measured beginning at age 25, when formal education is over for most people.[9] In addition to following previous educational attainment specifications, these age categories were also useful because migration increases and peaks between ages 18 and 24, before declining at age 25.

---

[9] "Even when data are collected from all household members regardless of age, the Census Bureau generally publishes data only for adults. Most publications focus on adults aged 25 years and over, when education has been completed for most people," U.S. Census Bureau, "About Educational Attainment," <www.census.gov/hhes/socdemo/education/about/index.html>.

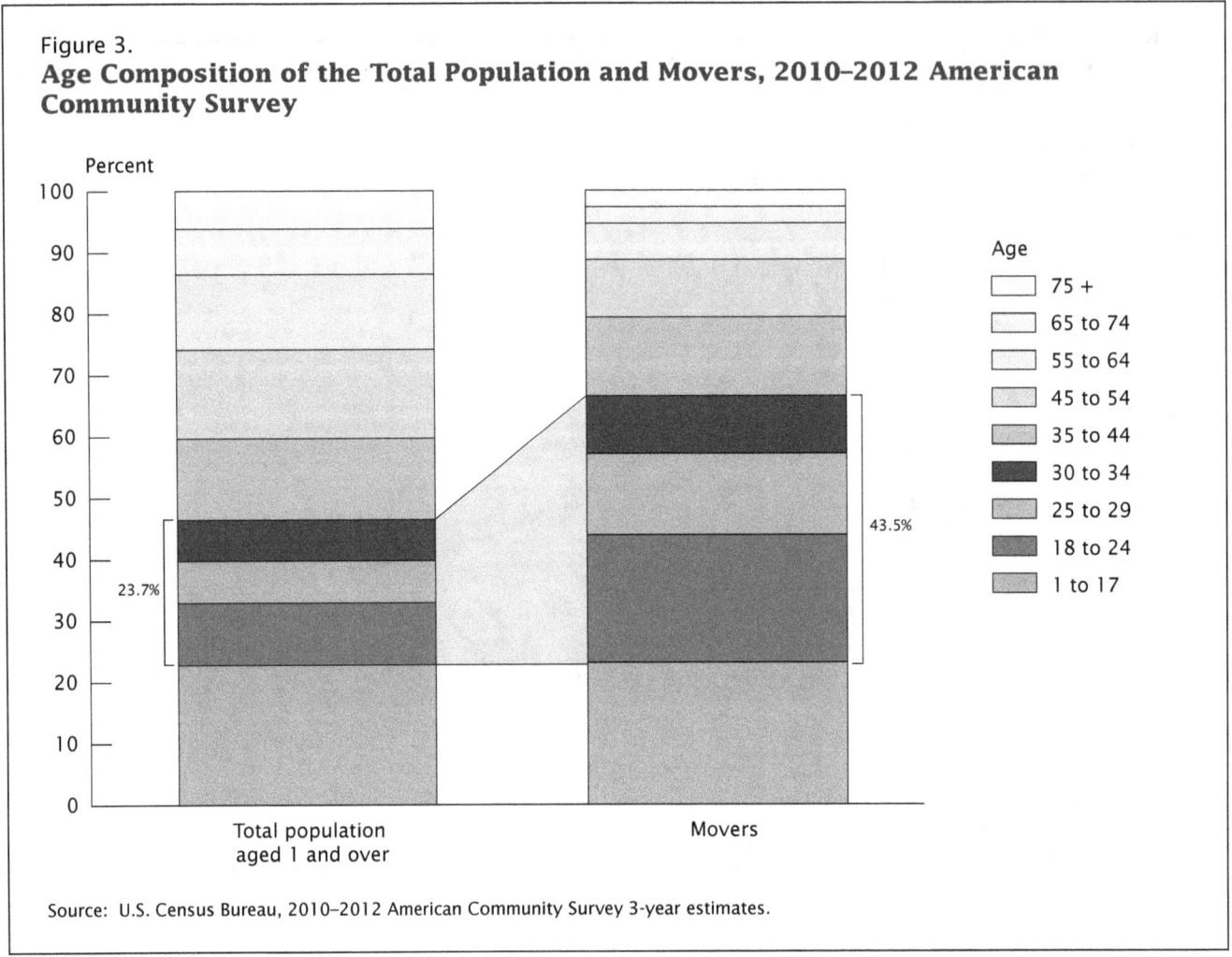

Figure 3.
Age Composition of the Total Population and Movers, 2010–2012 American Community Survey

Source: U.S. Census Bureau, 2010–2012 American Community Survey 3-year estimates.

People who lived in group quarters are a highly mobile population and were also overrepresented by young adults. About 2.6 percent of the total population lived in group quarters, compared with about 5.9 percent of young adults. Of those who lived in group quarters, 48.4 percent moved in the last year compared with those who lived in housing units who had a mover rate of 14.2 percent. Young adults who lived in group quarters also had a higher migration rate than those living in housing units, 58.0 percent compared with 25.9 percent (Table 1).

Presented in this report are migration rates across various demographic, socioeconomic, and family characteristics for all young adults, 18- to 24-year-olds, 25- to 29-year-olds, and 30- to 34-year-olds during the postrecession (2010–2012 ACS). In order to highlight how migration differed between the periods, the next section discusses the change in migration rates from the 2007–2009 recession period to the 2010–2012 postrecession period rather than the migration rates of the recession period. The last section examines inmovers by metro size.

YOUNG ADULT MIGRANTS' CHARACTERISTICS, POSTRECESSION, 2010–2012

Demographics

According to 2007–2009 ACS data, about 21 million young adults moved during this time period (Table 2). These young adults had a migration rate of about 29.2 percent, compared with 15.7 percent for the total population.[10] For the younger age group, those aged 18 to 24, the migration rate was about 33.3 percent, where migration

---

[10] The universe for 1-year migration rates includes anyone aged 1 or over.

Table 1.
Migration Rates for Housing Units and Group Quarters for Young Adults and the Total Population

Population	Total population		Total Young Adults	
	Migration rate (percent)	Margin of error	Migration rate (percent)	Margin of error
Housing unit...	14.2	0.1	25.9	0.1
Group quarters	48.4	0.2	58.0	0.3

Source: U.S. Census Bureau, 2010–2012 American Community Survey 3-year estimates.

peaked for young adults. Among 25- to 29-year-olds, the migration rate declined to 30.3 percent, and further declined to 21.8 percent for 30- to 34-year-olds. These rates change in the 2010–2012 postrecession period (Table 3), where the overall mover rate declined to 15.1 percent, and the rate for the Total Young Adult group went down to 27.8 percent.

Looking at differences by sex during the 2010–2012 postrecession period, the migration rates of males and females differed very little in the Total Young Adult population (Figure 4). Differences in sex became apparent when young adults were divided into the three age groups. Among 18- to 24-year-olds, females had a higher rate of migration than males (32.4 percent compared with 29.8 percent); but among 25- to 29-year-olds and 30- to 34-year-olds, the pattern reversed, and males were more likely to migrate than females (29.5 percent compared with 28.6 percent, and 22.5 percent compared with 20.4 percent, respectively).

Compared with White young adult movers, who had a migration rate of 28.0 percent, Black (27.4 percent), American Indian and Alaska Native (25.6 percent), and Some Other Race (24.2 percent) were less likely to move.[11,12] The remaining racial categories, Asian (29.8 percent), Native Hawaiian and Other Pacific Islander (29.7 percent), and Two or More Races (28.5 percent) were more likely to migrate than White, young adult movers. The same pattern was generally true for 18- to 24-year-olds and 25- to 29-year-olds as well. However, among 30- to 34-year-olds, Black, Asian, and Two or More Races movers

[11] Federal surveys now give respondents the option of reporting more than one race. Therefore, two basic ways of defining a race group are possible. A group such as Asian may be defined as those who reported Asian and no other race (the race-alone or single-race concept) or as those who reported Asian regardless of whether they also reported another race (the race-alone-or-in-combination concept). This report shows data using the first approach (race alone). Use of the single-race population does not imply that it is the preferred method of presenting or analyzing data. The Census Bureau uses a variety of approaches.
[12] All percentages are rates of migration, unless otherwise noted.

were among the highest migration rates (24.1, 24.6, and 23.9 percent, respectively), while White movers had the lowest (20.6 percent).[13]

A different story emerged when examining migration rates by Hispanic origin. Non-Hispanics were more likely to migrate than Hispanics; however, this was especially apparent in the 18- to 24-year-old age group, where 32.9 percent of young adult non-Hispanics migrated in the last year compared with 24.2 percent of Hispanics. The gap in migration rates decreased when the 25- to 29-year-old group was compared with the 30- to 34-year-old group.

The native born were more likely to migrate within the United States than foreign-born young adults.[14] This pattern changed among 30- to 34-year-olds, where the foreign born were more likely to migrate than

[13] Native Hawaiian and Pacific Islander was not statistically different from any other race category.
[14] The native born are more likely to migrate within or to the United States if they are coming from Puerto Rico.

Table 2.
Migration Rates by Selected Characteristics for Young Adults, Recession Years 2007–2009 ACS 3-Year Estimates

Characteristic	Total population aged 1 and over			Total Young Adults			Aged 18–24			Aged 25–29			Aged 30–34		
	Movers	Migration rate (percent)	Margin of error	Movers	Migration rate (percent)	Margin of error	Movers	Migration rate (percent)	Margin of error	Movers	Migration rate (percent)	Margin of error	Movers	Migration rate (percent)	Margin of error
Total.............	47,636,609	15.7	0.1	21,007,269	29.2	0.1	10,152,912	33.3	0.1	6,539,736	30.3	0.1	4,314,621	21.8	0.1
Sex															
Male..................	24,194,510	16.2	*0.1	10,773,437	29.3	*0.1	5,037,795	32.1	*0.2	3,433,471	31.1	*0.2	2,302,171	22.9	*0.2
Female................	23,442,099	15.2	†*0.1	10,233,832	29.1	†*0.1	5,115,117	34.6	†*0.2	3,106,265	29.4	†*0.2	2,012,450	20.6	†0.2
Race															
White alone...........	32,896,634	14.5	*0.1	14,957,166	29.4	*0.1	7,429,632	34.4	*0.1	4,623,797	30.3	*0.2	2,903,737	20.8	0.2
Black or African American alone	7,464,336	20.0	†*0.1	2,909,498	29.4	*0.2	1,362,142	30.7	†*0.3	904,171	31.1	†*0.4	643,185	25.4	†*0.3
American Indian and Alaska Native alone	453,704	18.8	†*0.4	184,900	28.6	†*0.7	90,547	30.5	†1.1	55,834	29.5	*1.1	38,519	23.9	†*1.3
Asian alone..........	2,285,053	17.1	†0.2	1,075,407	30.0	†0.3	418,862	33.4	†0.4	361,197	32.3	†*0.5	295,348	24.4	†0.4
Native Hawaiian and Other Pacific Islander alone	96,809	21.4	†1.0	43,435	30.8	1.5	21,059	33.6	2.0	12,745	30.8	3.1	9,631	26.1	†2.5
Some Other Race alone	3,004,947	18.5	†*0.2	1,309,318	25.5	†*0.3	550,645	27.5	†*0.4	432,016	27.0	†*0.5	326,657	21.4	†0.4
Two or More Races	1,435,126	20.3	†*0.2	527,545	30.4	†*0.4	280,025	33.3	†*0.6	149,976	30.9	†*0.8	97,544	23.8	†0.8
Hispanic Origin															
Hispanic or Latino......	8,566,090	17.2	*0.1	3,525,000	24.5	*0.2	1,513,758	26.2	*0.2	1,151,017	26.2	*0.3	860,225	20.4	0.2
Not Hispanic or Latino...	39,070,519	15.4	†*0.1	17,482,269	30.4	†*0.1	8,639,154	34.9	†*0.1	5,388,719	31.3	†*0.1	3,454,396	22.2	†*0.2
Nativity and Citizenship															
Native................	41,082,609	15.5	*0.1	17,907,289	29.6	*0.1	9,089,590	33.5	*0.1	5,453,669	30.5	*0.2	3,364,030	21.6	*0.1
Foreign born..........	6,554,000	17.2	†*0.1	3,099,980	27.4	†*0.2	1,063,322	31.7	†*0.3	1,086,067	29.3	†*0.3	950,591	22.2	†0.3
Naturalized citizen ...	1,638,505	10.0	0.1	571,148	20.5	*0.3	185,969	24.7	*0.5	197,840	23.1	*0.5	187,339	16.0	*0.4
Noncitizen...........	4,915,495	22.6	†*0.2	2,528,832	29.6	†*0.2	877,353	33.7	†*0.4	888,227	31.2	†*0.3	763,252	24.6	†0.3
Educational Attainment[1]															
Less than high school	4,465,675	14.4	*0.1	2,881,669	27.1	*0.2	1,389,895	27.2	*0.2	851,872	29.9	*0.4	639,902	23.9	*0.3
High school graduate or equivalent..........	7,322,074	12.5	†*0.2	5,636,578	28.1	†*0.1	2,944,380	30.9	†*0.2	1,593,714	28.4	†*0.2	1,098,484	22.2	†*0.2
Some college..........	7,517,715	13.2	†*0.2	7,818,713	30.3	†*0.1	4,590,549	35.0	†*0.2	1,989,352	29.4	†*0.2	1,238,812	21.0	†*0.2
Bachelor's degree or higher.	7,066,992	12.6	†*0.6	4,670,309	30.3	†*0.2	1,228,088	44.5	†*0.3	2,104,798	33.0	†*0.2	1,337,423	21.3	†0.2
Employment status															
Employed, at work.....	21,759,904	15.5	*0.1	13,278,475	27.9	*0.1	5,651,781	33.0	*0.1	4,628,768	29.5	*0.2	2,997,926	20.4	*0.1
Employed, with a job but not at work............	620,385	16.6	†*0.2	372,784	29.7	†*0.5	167,138	37.4	†*0.8	120,964	30.0	0.9	84,682	20.9	0.7
Unemployed...........	2,796,824	23.6	†*0.2	1,735,684	30.5	†*0.3	945,668	30.6	†*0.3	483,293	32.2	†*0.4	306,723	27.9	†*0.5
Armed Forces, at work ...	572,208	48.5	†*0.6	481,755	56.0	†*0.7	291,302	65.9	†1.1	125,440	50.0	†1.0	65,013	38.9	†1.3
Armed Forces, with a job but not at work...........	7,916	54.6	†*4.9	6,942	54.9	†*5.0	4,773	56.1	†*6.7	1,287	52.7	†10.3	882	52.3	†12.4
Not in the labor force....	11,845,660	14.0	†*0.1	5,131,629	31.0	†*0.2	3,092,250	32.9	†*0.2	1,179,984	31.4	†*0.3	859,395	25.2	†*0.3

See footnotes at end of table.

Table 2.
Migration Rates by Selected Characteristics for Young Adults, Recession Years 2007–2009 ACS 3-Year Estimates—Con.

Characteristic	Total population aged 1 and over			Total Young Adults			Aged 18–24			Aged 25–29			Aged 30–34		
	Movers	Migration rate (percent)	Margin of error	Movers	Migration rate (percent)	Margin of error	Movers	Migration rate (percent)	Margin of error	Movers	Migration rate (percent)	Margin of error	Movers	Migration rate (percent)	Margin of error
Mean annual adjusted personal income (in dollars)	$20,631	X	$64	$21,074	X	$61	$12,185	X	$52	$27,117	X	$117	$32,832	X	$186
Marital Status															
Married	12,488,844	10.2	*0.1	5,495,392	24.8	*0.1	1,328,643	42.4	*0.3	2,185,556	27.1	*0.2	1,981,193	18.0	0.2
Widowed	1,423,797	9.3	†*0.1	37,979	29.3	†1.2	8,142	32.5	†2.9	13,133	32.1	†2.9	16,704	26.3	†1.9
Separated	4,553,031	17.5	†*0.1	968,515	34.9	†*0.3	109,572	46.9	†*1.2	369,654	39.2	†*0.5	489,289	30.6	†*0.4
Divorced	1,474,293	27.4	†*0.2	523,318	40.8	†*0.5	96,151	46.8	†1.0	201,961	42.7	†*0.9	225,206	37.3	†*0.6
Never married	27,696,644	20.4	†*0.1	13,982,065	30.7	†*0.1	8,610,404	32.0	†*0.1	3,769,432	31.2	†*0.2	1,602,229	24.4	†*0.2
Own Children Under 18															
Not present	19,723,918	14.1	†*0.1	11,082,219	31.7	†*0.1	5,580,136	35.0	†*0.1	3,696,343	31.9	†*0.2	1,805,740	24.4	†*0.2
Present	23,786,442	15.2	0.1	7,387,836	22.5	0.1	2,619,509	23.0	0.1	2,504,326	26.5	0.2	2,264,001	18.9	0.2
Presence of children under 6 only	6,974,929	22.8	*0.2	3,473,371	27.9	*0.2	1,403,658	38.3	*0.4	1,275,118	27.8	*0.3	794,595	18.8	*0.3
Presence of children 6–17 only	9,678,070	11.5	†*0.1	2,004,227	17.1	†*0.2	791,220	13.2	†*0.2	479,953	24.0	†*0.4	733,054	19.8	†*0.3
Presence of children under 6 and 6–17 years	7,133,443	17.1	†*0.2	1,910,238	22.0	†*0.2	424,631	24.1	†*0.4	749,255	26.2	†*0.3	736,352	18.2	†0.3

† Significant at the 90 percent confidence level within category, using first category as reference group.
* Significant at the 90 percent confidence level between the 2007–2009 ACS 3-year estimates and the 2010–2012 ACS 3-year estimates.
X Not applicable.
[1] Educational attainment for the total population restricts the universe to those aged 25 and older. For age groups <18 years, total young, and 18–24 years, the restriction is lifted.
Source: U.S. Census Bureau, 2007–2009 American Community Survey 3-year estimates.

Table 3.

Migration Rates By Selected Characteristics For Young Adults, Postrecession Years 2010–2012

Characteristic	Total population Aged 1 and over			Total Young Adults			Aged 18–24			Aged 25–29			Aged 30–34		
	Movers	Migration rate (percent)	Margin of error	Movers	Migration rate (percent)	Margin of error	Movers	Migration rate (percent)	Margin of error	Movers	Migration rate (percent)	Margin of error	Movers	Migration rate (percent)	Margin of error
Total	47,086,720	15.1	0.1	20,463,254	27.8	0.1	9,785,234	31.1	0.1	6,224,492	29.0	0.1	4,453,528	21.5	0.1
Sex															
Male	23,654,016	15.5	*0.1	10,329,019	27.7	*0.1	4,799,498	29.8	*0.2	3,189,352	29.5	*0.2	2,340,169	22.5	*0.1
Female	23,432,704	14.8	†0.1	10,134,235	27.9	†0.1	4,985,736	32.4	†*0.1	3,035,140	28.6	†*0.2	2,113,359	20.4	†0.1
Race															
White alone	32,303,395	14.0	*0.1	14,431,810	28.0	*0.1	7,013,144	32.2	*0.1	4,399,233	29.1	*0.1	3,019,433	20.6	0.1
Black or African American alone	7,272,992	18.7	†0.1	2,807,695	27.4	†*0.2	1,331,803	28.3	†*0.2	822,188	29.2	†*0.4	653,704	24.1	†*0.3
American Indian and Alaska Native alone	440,288	17.4	†*0.4	171,431	25.6	†*0.6	83,357	27.2	†*0.8	49,204	26.3	†*1.0	38,870	22.0	†*1.0
Asian alone	2,539,245	16.9	†0.2	1,222,377	29.8	†0.3	509,624	32.8	†0.4	396,650	31.4	†0.5	316,103	24.6	†0.4
Native Hawaiian and Other Pacific Islander alone	111,311	21.5	†1.0	47,945	29.7	†1.3	22,930	33.1	†2.0	15,076	31.3	2.3	9,939	22.8	2.3
Some Other Race alone	2,663,871	17.9	†*0.2	1,133,460	24.2	†*0.3	485,565	24.9	†*0.4	360,940	26.0	†*0.5	286,955	21.3	†0.4
Two or More races	1,755,618	19.7	†*0.2	648,536	28.5	†*0.3	338,811	30.0	†*0.5	181,201	29.8	†*0.7	128,524	23.9	†0.6
Hispanic Origin															
Hispanic or Latino	9,046,344	16.6	*0.1	3,666,329	23.3	*0.2	1,621,639	24.2	*0.2	1,142,206	25.1	*0.2	902,484	20.2	0.2
Not Hispanic or Latino	38,040,376	14.8	†*0.1	16,796,925	29.0	†*0.1	8,163,595	32.9	†*0.1	5,082,286	30.1	†*0.1	3,551,044	21.8	†*0.1
Nativity and Citizenship															
Native	40,448,986	14.9	*0.1	17,453,964	28.0	*0.1	8,760,338	31.2	*0.1	5,182,400	29.2	*0.1	3,511,226	21.3	*0.1
Foreign born	6,637,734	16.4	†*0.1	3,009,290	26.8	†*0.2	1,024,896	30.4	†*0.2	1,042,092	28.5	†*0.3	942,302	22.4	†0.3
Naturalized citizen	1,817,152	10.0	0.1	589,799	20.1	*0.3	179,936	22.7	*0.5	205,253	22.0	*0.5	204,610	17.0	*0.4
Noncitizen	4,820,582	21.5	†*0.1	2,419,491	29.1	†*0.2	844,960	32.8	†*0.4	836,839	30.7	†*0.3	737,692	24.5	†0.3
Educational Attainment[1]															
Less than high school	16,113,232	15.3	*0.1	2,533,880	25.0	*0.2	1,213,646	24.5	*0.3	709,412	28.1	*0.3	610,822	23.1	*0.3
High school graduate or equivalent	9,614,174	14.0	†*0.2	5,010,665	25.8	†*0.1	2,584,113	28.0	†*0.2	1,375,207	26.3	†*0.2	1,051,345	21.1	†*0.2
Some college	12,712,217	17.0	†*0.1	8,094,904	29.1	†*0.1	4,748,085	33.0	†*0.2	1,982,031	28.1	†*0.2	1,364,788	21.3	†*0.2
Bachelor's degree or higher	8,647,097	13.8	†*0.6	4,823,805	29.7	†*0.1	1,239,390	42.5	†*0.3	2,157,842	32.6	†*0.2	1,426,573	21.3	†0.2
Employment Status															
Employed, at work	20,668,956	14.9	*0.1	12,384,842	26.8	*0.1	5,094,719	31.2	*0.1	4,287,424	28.5	*0.1	3,002,699	20.1	*0.1
Employed, with a job but not at work	508,851	16.1	†*0.2	288,742	28.3	†*0.2	117,429	34.4	†*0.9	97,121	29.4	1.0	74,192	21.3	0.8
Unemployed	3,490,376	21.6	†*0.1	2,127,473	28.3	†*0.1	1,109,714	28.4	†*0.2	591,080	29.9	†*0.4	426,679	26.2	†*0.3
Armed Forces, at work	483,440	47.5	†*0.6	412,082	54.3	†*0.8	242,588	62.7	†*1.0	110,690	49.0	†1.1	58,804	40.4	†1.3
Armed Forces, with a job but not at work	5,068	49.2	†5.4	4,830	51.4	†5.6	3,587	52.7	†5.9	886	47.8	†11.3	357	48.1	†21.1
Not in the labor force	12,090,356	13.4	†*0.1	5,245,285	29.0	†*0.1	3,217,197	30.5	†*0.1	1,137,291	29.5	†*0.2	890,797	24.1	†*0.2

See footnotes at end of table.

Table 3.
Migration Rates By Selected Characteristics For Young Adults, Postrecession Years 2010-2012—Con.

Characteristic	Total population Aged 1 and over			Total Young Adults			Aged 18–24			Aged 25–29			Aged 30–34		
	Movers	Migration rate (percent)	Margin of error	Movers	Migration rate (percent)	Margin of error	Movers	Migration rate (percent)	Margin of error	Movers	Migration rate (percent)	Margin of error	Movers	Migration rate (percent)	Margin of error
Mean annual adjusted personal income (in dollars)	$20,611	X	$61.5	$20,462	X	$65.2	$10,978	X	$58.3	$26,856	X	$129.5	$32,363	X	$197.7
Marital Status															
Married	11,954,400	9.8	*0.0	5,001,387	24.0	*0.1	1,073,916	40.5	*0.4	1,959,398	26.8	*0.2	1,968,073	18.1	0.2
Widowed	1,359,579	8.9	†0.1	33,205	28.8	†1.5	6,178	37.3	4.4	10,930	32.3	†2.5	16,097	24.8	†2.1
Separated	4,612,581	16.5	†0.1	887,336	32.9	†0.3	87,007	41.9	†1.0	311,340	36.2	†0.5	488,989	30.0	†0.4
Divorced	1,467,832	26.0	†0.2	470,440	38.7	†0.5	79,790	46.2	†1.7	174,494	40.7	†0.8	216,156	35.3	†0.7
Never married	27,692,328	19.7	†0.1	14,070,886	28.8	†0.1	8,538,343	30.0	†0.1	3,768,330	29.4	†0.1	1,764,213	23.3	†0.2
Own Children Under 18															
Not present	19,760,597	13.5	†0.1	10,805,980	30.0	0.1	5,325,846	32.6	0.2	3,611,181	30.6	†0.1	1,868,953	23.7	†0.2
Present	23,428,780	14.9	*0.1	7,133,663	21.4	0.1	2,496,191	21.1	0.2	2,301,742	25.4	*0.2	2,335,730	18.9	0.2
Presence of children under 6 only	6,778,887	22.3	*0.2	3,327,931	26.8	*0.2	1,270,055	35.4	*0.4	1,211,944	27.1	*0.3	845,932	19.3	*0.2
Presence of children 6–17 only	9,574,904	11.4	†0.1	1,943,225	16.3	†0.2	806,539	12.7	†0.2	422,135	22.4	†0.4	714,551	19.2	*0.3
Presence of children under 6 and 6–17 years	7,074,989	16.6	†0.2	1,862,507	21.0	†0.2	419,597	21.6	†0.4	667,663	24.8	†0.3	775,247	18.2	†0.2

† Significant at the 90 percent confidence level within category, using first category as reference group.
* Significant at the 90 percent confidence level between the 2007–2009 ACS 3-year estimates and the 2010–2012 ACS 3-Year Estimates.
X Not applicable.
¹ Educational attainment for the total population restricts the universe to those aged 25 and older. For age groups <18 years, Total young, and 18–24 years, the restriction is lifted.
Source: U.S. Census Bureau, 2010–2012 American Community Survey 3-year estimates.

natives. Among the foreign born, migration rates across citizenship status vary greatly. About 29.1 percent of all young adults without citizenship moved in the last year, compared with 20.1 percent of all foreign-born young adults with citizenship. The difference was more apparent for 18- to 24-year-olds, where 32.9 percent of young adults without citizenship moved in the last year, while only about 22.7 percent of young adults with citizenship moved. Noncitizens had higher migration rates than foreign-born citizens for 25- to 29-year-olds and 30- to 34-year-olds.

Socioeconomic indicators

Educational attainment had a clear association with the likelihood to migrate. Among all young adults, those who had some college or graduated from college were the most likely to move (Figure 5). Measuring educational attainment across age groups was not ideal as many 18- to 24-year-olds are still enrolled in school.[15] However, this age group continued to have some of the highest migration rates, especially among college graduates. For the 25- to 29-year-olds, college graduates continued to be the most likely to move (32.6 percent), while those aged 30 to 34 with less than a high school degree were most likely to move (23.1 percent).

Migration rates varied depending on employment status. Young adults most likely to migrate were those who reported that they were

[15] "Even when data are collected from all household members regardless of age, the Census Bureau generally publishes data only for adults. Most publications focus on adults aged 25 years and over, when education has been completed for most people," U.S. Census Bureau, "About Educational Attainment," <www.census.gov/hhes/socdemo/education/about/index.html>.

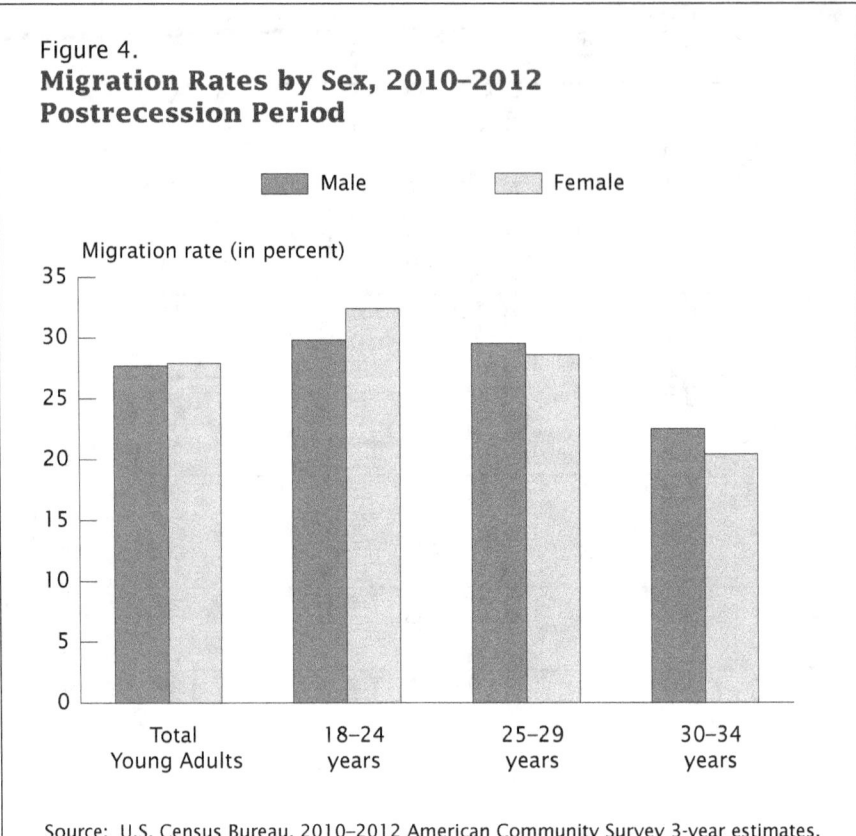

Figure 4.
Migration Rates by Sex, 2010–2012 Postrecession Period

Source: U.S. Census Bureau, 2010–2012 American Community Survey 3-year estimates.

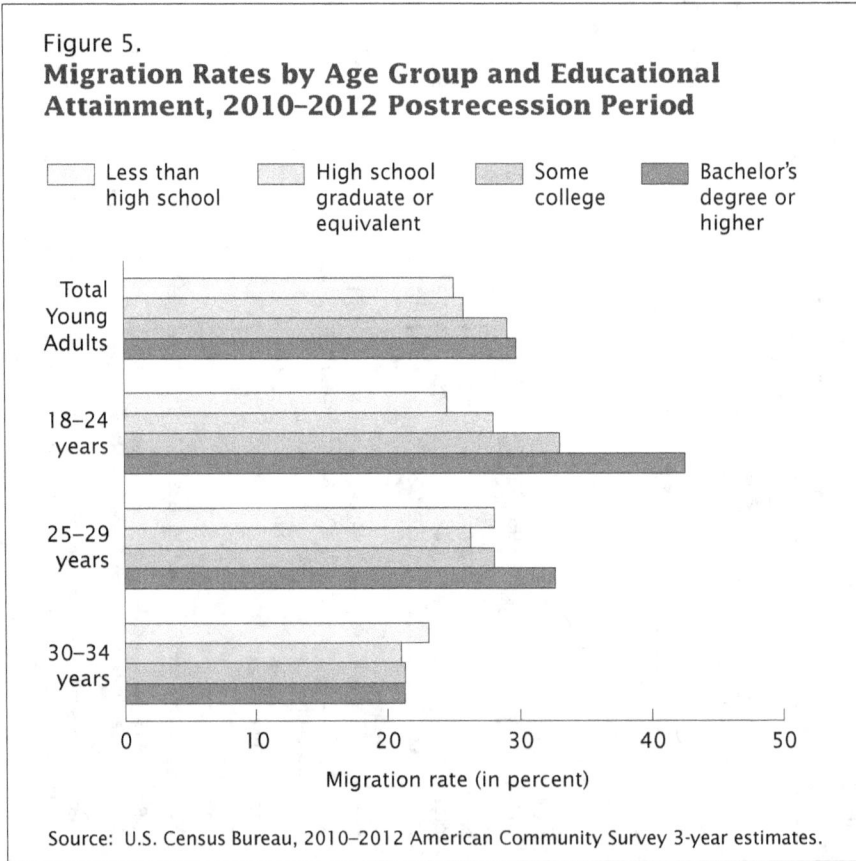

Figure 5.
Migration Rates by Age Group and Educational Attainment, 2010–2012 Postrecession Period

Source: U.S. Census Bureau, 2010–2012 American Community Survey 3-year estimates.

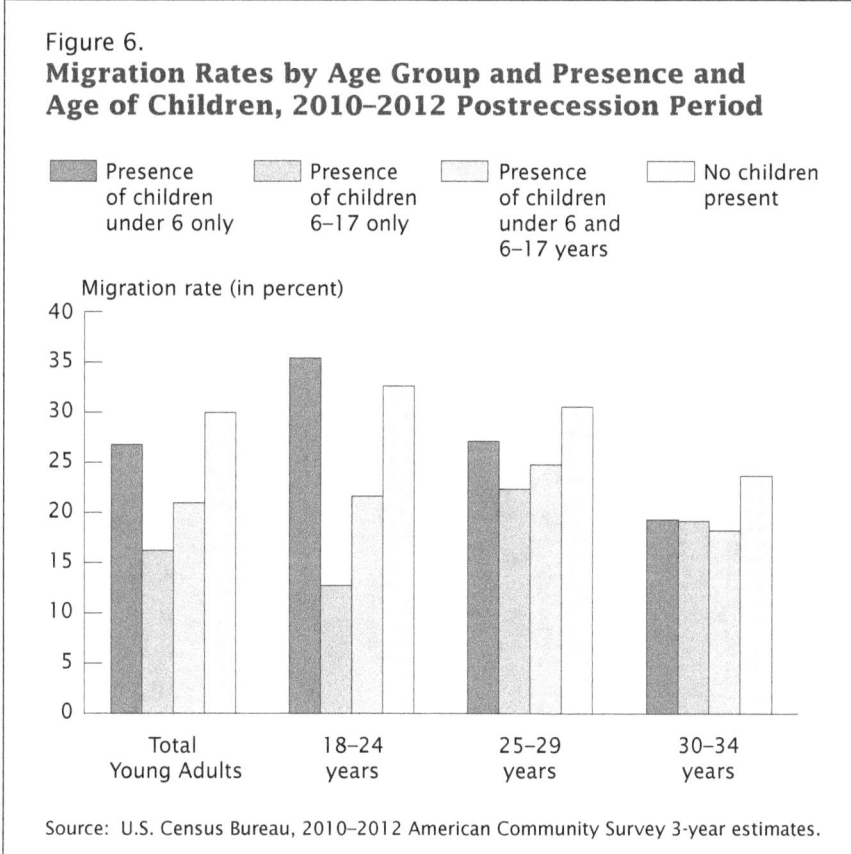

Figure 6.
Migration Rates by Age Group and Presence and Age of Children, 2010–2012 Postrecession Period

- Presence of children under 6 only
- Presence of children 6–17 only
- Presence of children under 6 and 6–17 years
- No children present

Migration rate (in percent)

Source: U.S. Census Bureau, 2010–2012 American Community Survey 3-year estimates.

Armed Forces, at work and not at work, (54.3 percent and 51.4 percent).[16,17] This was expected as they are known to be a highly mobile population.[18] Those who were employed, at work were least likely to have moved, as expected.

The migration rates of this group declined with each age category. For example, those aged 30 to 34 years who reported being employed and at work had the lowest migration rate (20.1 percent), likely because many had settled into a job or career and had no need to relocate.[19]

Family characteristics

When marital status was examined, those who reported being separated or divorced had the highest rates of migration for all young adults. Generally, single young adults had higher migration rates than their married peers. Married young adults had the lowest migration rates across all age groups except those aged 18 to 24, though this may be due in part to a relatively small sample size of widowed, separated,

and divorced people of this age. For the older age groups, the migration pattern for marital status looked similar to that for the Total Young Adult group.

Many people move into larger homes or change school districts around the time a child is born or a few years later.[20] In general, young adults were more likely to move if there were no children present in the household. However, the age of the child had an effect on the likelihood of moving as well.

If the respondent's own children were reported as present in the home, the Census Bureau aggregates them into two age categories to better interpret school transitions: Under 6 years old and between 6 and 17 years old.[21] The assumption is that many children under the age of 6 were not enrolled in school, while children aged 6 to 17 were enrolled. Young adults were less likely to move if all of their children were school-aged (Figure 6). Those 18 to 24 years old with only a child(ren) under 6 were the most likely to move, while those with a child(ren) between the ages of 6 and 17 were the least likely to move. Young adults between 25 and 29 years of age had similar migration patterns to the overall young adult population. For young adults aged 30 to 34, age of the child(ren) present appeared to have less of an effect on migration than for the younger age groups.

[16] See ACS subject definitions of employment status. Those who were "Employed" or were working for the Armed Forces could be "at work" or "with a job but not at work." "At work" includes those who did any work at all during the reference week as paid employees, worked in their own business or profession, worked on their own farm, or worked 15 hours or more as unpaid workers on a family farm or in a family business. "With a job but not at work" includes those who did not work during the reference week but had jobs or businesses from which they were temporarily absent due to illness, bad weather, industrial dispute, vacation, or other personal reasons. See <www.census .gov/acs/www/Downloads/data_documentation /SubjectDefinitions/2012_ACSSubject Definitions.pdf>.
[17] The estimates for "Armed Forces, at work" and "Armed Forces, not at work" were not statistically different from one another.
[18] Melanie A. Rapino and Julia Beckhusen, "The Migration of Military Spouses using the 2007–2011 5-Year American Community Survey," Working Paper No. 2013-25, U.S. Census Bureau, Washington, DC, 2012.

[19] David K. Irhke and Carol S. Faber, "Geographical Mobility: 2005 to 2010," *Current Population Reports*, P20-567, U.S. Census Bureau, Washington, DC, 2012.

[20] Sandra E. Black, "Do Better Schools Matter? Parental Valuation of Elementary Education," *Quarterly Journal of Economics*, May 1999, 114(2), pp. 577–99.
[21] A third category allows for having at least one child under 6, as well as, at least one child between 6 and 17 years.

CHANGES IN MIGRATION RATES FROM THE 2007–2009 RECESSION PERIOD TO THE 2010–2012 POSTRECESSION PERIOD

Migration slowed in the years after the recession for young adults (Figure 7). Migration rates for the 2007–2009 recession period across demographic, economic, and household indicators were mostly higher than migration rates in the postrecession period of 2010–2012. The differences in migration rates between periods were larger for 18- to 24-year-olds (–2.2 percentage points) than for the other age groups. The following sections discuss these differences in migration rates between the recession and postrecession period in more detail.

Demographics

From the recession period (2007–2009) to the postrecession period (2010–2012), young adult males had a larger decline in migration rates than females (Figure 8). The differences by sex were particularly apparent for the 25- to 29-year-old age group, where the migration rate for men declined 1.6 percentage points, but only about half as much for women (–0.8 percentage points). The declines in migration rates for those aged 18 to 24 and 30 to 34 were similar for males and females.

Examining migration and race, the American Indian and Alaska Native alone group had among the largest decline in migration among the Total Young Adult group (Figure 9).[22] Among the 25- to 29-year-old age group, Native Hawaiian and Other Pacific Islander appeared to be the only group to

[22] Black and Native Hawaiian or Pacific Islander were not statistically different.

Figure 7.

Migration Rates by Age Group for the 2007–2009 Recession and 2010–2012 Postrecession Periods

Source: U.S. Census Bureau, 2007–2009 and 2010–2012 American Community Survey 3-year estimates.

Figure 8.

Migration Rate Difference Between 2007–2009 Recession and 2010–2012 Postrecession Periods by Age Group and Sex

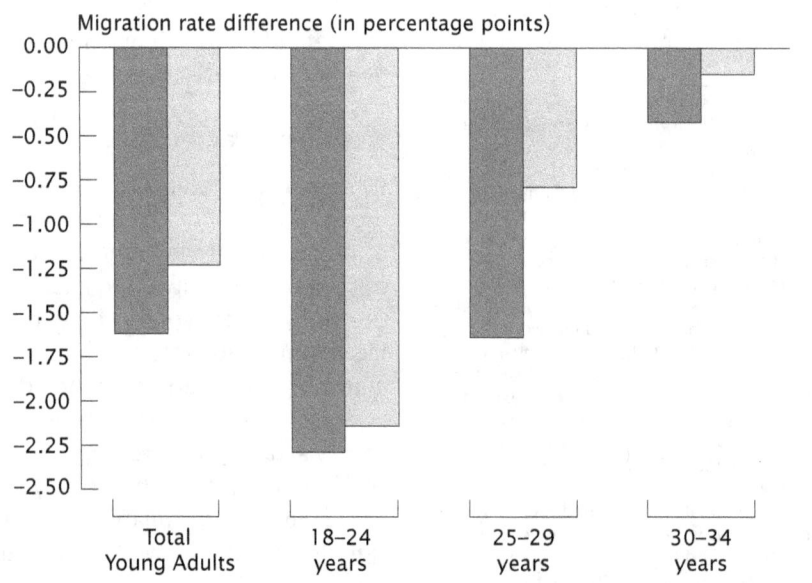

Source: U.S. Census Bureau, 2007–2009 and 2010–2012 American Community Survey 3-year estimates.

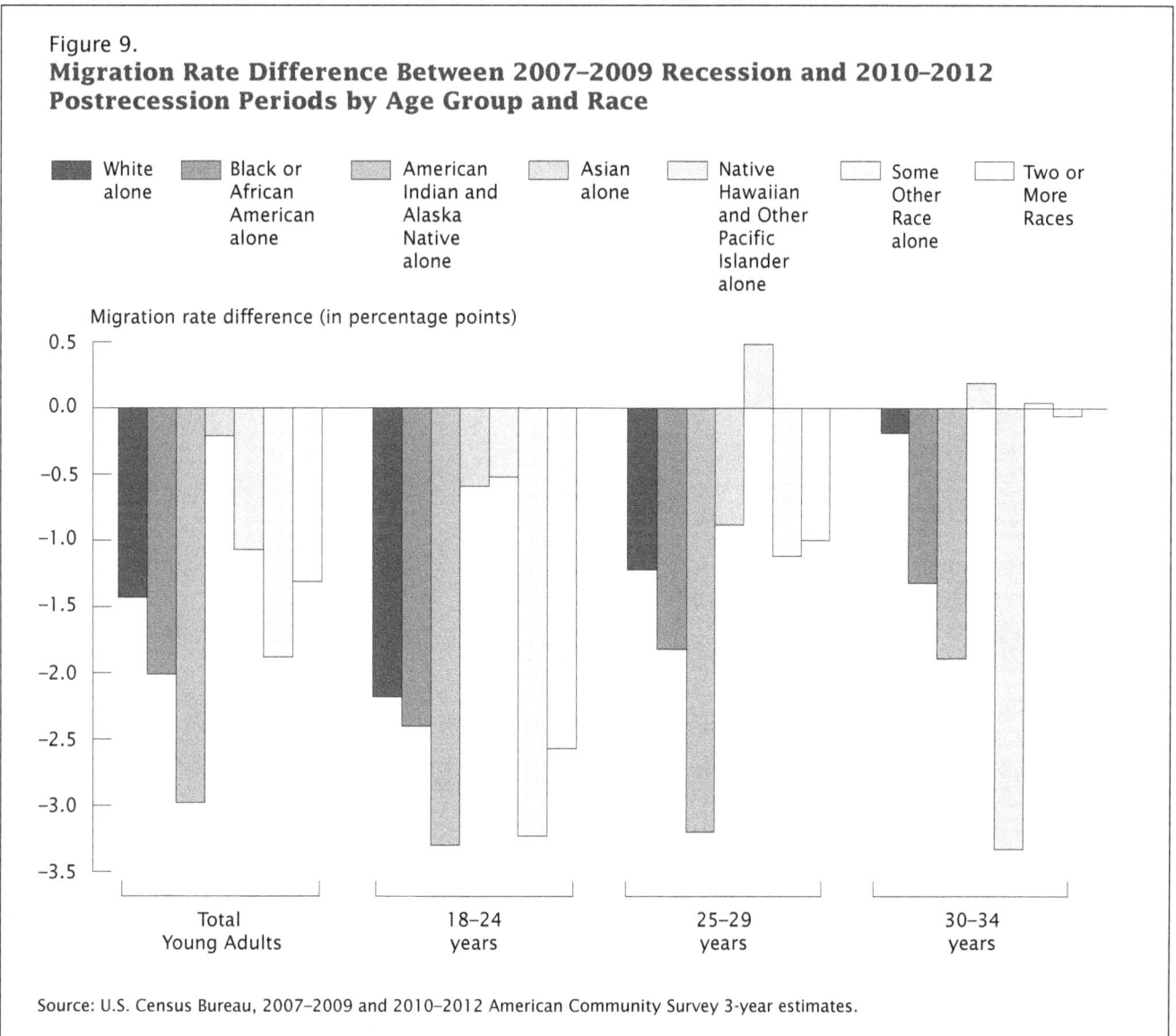

Figure 9.
Migration Rate Difference Between 2007–2009 Recession and 2010–2012 Postrecession Periods by Age Group and Race

- White alone
- Black or African American alone
- American Indian and Alaska Native alone
- Asian alone
- Native Hawaiian and Other Pacific Islander alone
- Some Other Race alone
- Two or More Races

Migration rate difference (in percentage points)

Total Young Adults | 18–24 years | 25–29 years | 30–34 years

Source: U.S. Census Bureau, 2007–2009 and 2010–2012 American Community Survey 3-year estimates.

have an increase in their migration rates, however this increase was not statistically significant when compared with the other races. For the 30- to-34-year-olds, the apparent increase in migration for Asians was also not statistically significant.

Hispanic origin was a significant factor in migration likelihood. Overall, non-Hispanics had a higher migration rate than Hispanics both during the recession period and in the postrecession period (Tables 1 and 2). However, the migration rate of Hispanics declined by about 1.2 percentage points and about 1.4 percentage points for non-Hispanics. Migration rates declined by about 2.0 percentage points among 18- to 24-year-olds for both Hispanics and non-Hispanics.

Comparing movers who were foreign born and those who were native born, the native born had higher migration rates in the recession period as well as the postrecession period. The native born also experienced a larger decline in migration rate across all age groups. The migration rate for foreign-born citizens was lower than the rate of those who were not citizens in both periods, while 18- to 24-year-old foreign-born citizens experienced a larger decline compared with noncitizens. Among 30- to 34-year-olds, foreign-born citizens were more likely to move in the postrecession period than the recession period compared to their noncitizen peers.

Socioeconomic indicators

Many young adults move to go to college or for a job. Declining rates in migration from the recession period to the postrecession period may indicate that young adults were choosing colleges and jobs closer to home so they do not have to move (Figure 10). They also may be foregoing college altogether or are unable to find jobs. Among 18- to 24-year-olds, those with at least some college had the smallest declines in migration compared to those who did not go to college. College graduates aged 25 to 29 experienced the smallest decline in migration while 30- to 34-year-olds with some college experience had an increase in migration rates from the 2007–2009 recession period to the 2010–2012 postrecession period.

We further examined the roll of education in young migrants' lives through school enrollment and group quarters (GQ) status.[23] Young migrants, especially those in the 18 to 24 years of age category, were more likely to be enrolled in school and living in or out of a GQ than 25- to 29-year-olds and 30- to-34 year olds in both the 2007–2009 recession period and the 2010–2012 postrecession period. Figure 11 shows the percentage of

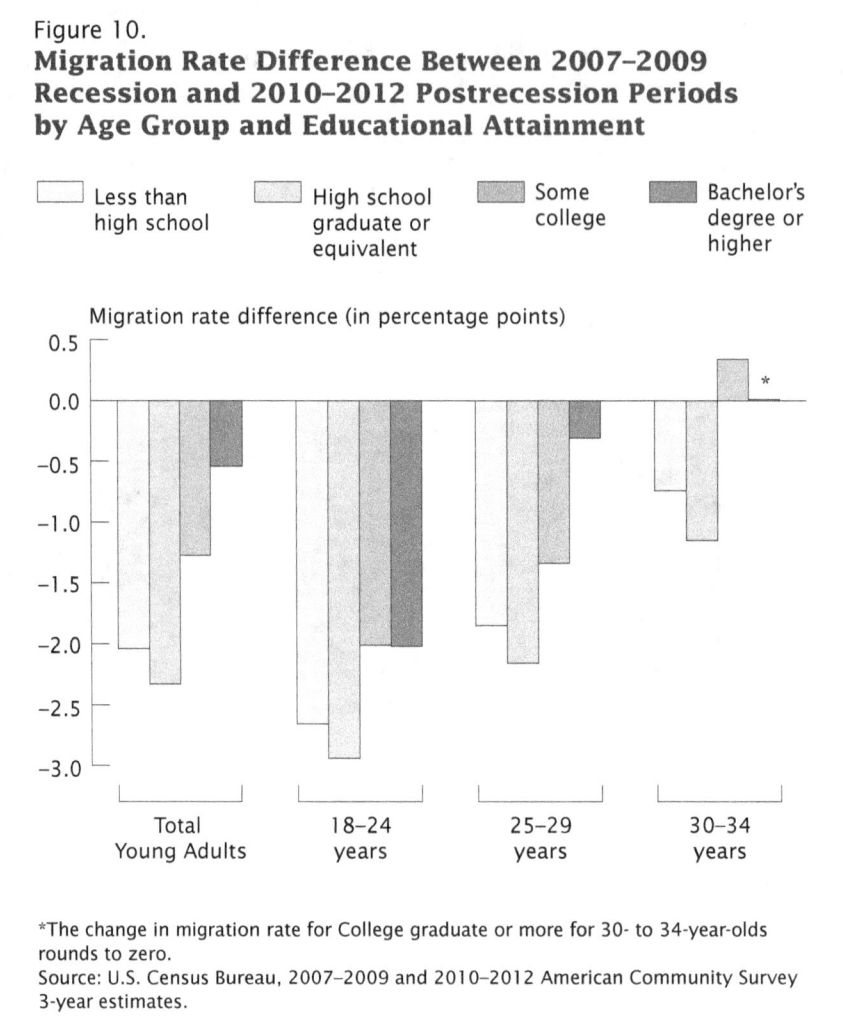

Figure 10.
Migration Rate Difference Between 2007–2009 Recession and 2010–2012 Postrecession Periods by Age Group and Educational Attainment

☐ Less than high school ☐ High school graduate or equivalent ☐ Some college ■ Bachelor's degree or higher

Migration rate difference (in percentage points)

*The change in migration rate for College graduate or more for 30- to 34-year-olds rounds to zero.
Source: U.S. Census Bureau, 2007–2009 and 2010–2012 American Community Survey 3-year estimates.

[23] American Community Survey Subject Definitions: "A group quarters is a place where people live or stay, in a group living arrangement, that is owned or managed by an entity or organization providing housing and/or services for the residents. This is not a typical household-type living arrangement. These services may include custodial or medical care as well as other types of assistance, and residency is commonly restricted to those receiving these services. People living in group quarters are usually not related to each other. Group quarters include such places as college residence halls, residential treatment centers, skilled nursing facilities, group homes, military barracks, correctional facilities, and workers' dormitories." See <www.census.gov/acs/www/Downloads/data_documentation/GroupDefinitions/2012GQ_Definitions.pdf>.

young migrants who lived in a GQ that reported being enrolled or not enrolled in school at the time of survey.[24] The results for recession versus postrecession were similar, but there are some statistically significant differences to note. The percentage of migrants enrolled in school for 18- to 24-year-olds increased in the postrecession years for those residing in a GQ and those not residing in a GQ, 8.1 to 8.3 and 42.2 to 43.8 percent, respectively. Additionally, there was

[24] Figure 11 shows percentages, not mover rates.

an increase in the percentage of 25- to 29-year-olds and 30- to 34-year-olds enrolled in school not living in a GQ in the postrecession years (15.5 to 17.0 percent and 9.0 to 10.0 percent, respectively). One possible explanation for this may be that continuing or furthering education may have been a result of a decrease in the number of available jobs in the recession years and additionally, students over 24 may forgo living on campus in lieu of living in their own home or with others.

Figure 11.
Young Adult Movers by Age Group, School Enrollment Status, and Group Quarters (GQ) Status for 2007–2009 Recession and 2010–2012 Postrecession Periods

Legend:
- Not enrolled, not in GQ
- Not enrolled, in GQ
- Enrolled, not in GQ
- Enrolled, in GQ

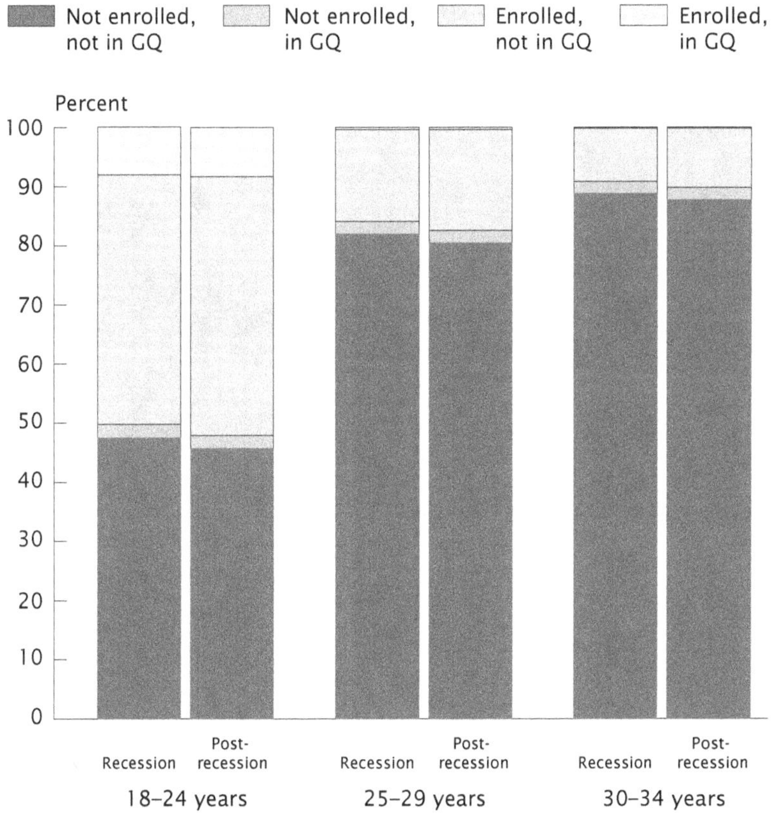

Source: U.S. Census Bureau, 2007–2009 and 2010–2012 American Community Survey 3-year estimates.

Evidence for this was seen in 30- to 34-year-olds with children, as their migration rate from the recession to postrecession period had almost no change. Young adults aged 30 to 34 with children under 6 experienced increased migration between periods, while 18- to 24-year-olds with a child(ren) under 6 had the largest decline in migration compared with other young adults across age groups (Figure 13).[26]

METROPOLITAN AND MICROPOLITAN STATISTICAL AREAS

Metropolitan (metro) and *micropolitan (micro)* areas are geographic entities defined by the Office of Management and Budget (OMB). Collectively, metro and micro areas are referred to as Core Based Statistical Areas (CBSA).

A metro area contains an urban core area of 50,000 or more people. A micro area contains a core urban area of at least 10,000 people, but less than 50,000. Each CBSA is composed of one or more counties that contain the urban core. Additionally, any adjacent counties that are socially or economically integrated, (as measured by commuting to work) are included.

Given the recession, many people's employment statuses changed. Though this report only looks at change in the aggregate and does not track individuals, we may still assume that migration was affected by these employment status differences across periods. Generally, employed persons at work had smaller declines in migration rate except compared to those in the Armed Forces (Figure 12). No employment category across any age group experienced statistically significant increases in migration from recession to postrecession periods.

FAMILY CHARACTERISTICS

Migration rates by marital status were also expected to show declines. Married young adults experienced less of a decline in migration rate compared to other single young adults.[25] For presence of children, interestingly, the declines in migration were slightly steeper for young adults without children (–1.7 percentage points) than for young adults with children (–1.1 percentage points).

[25] Again, the data for young adults who are widowed have a relatively low sample size and therefore the increased rate of migration for this group was not statistically different from young adults who are married.

[26] Not statistically different from 18- to 24-year-olds with a child under 6 and a child aged 6–17, or 18- to 24-year-olds without children.

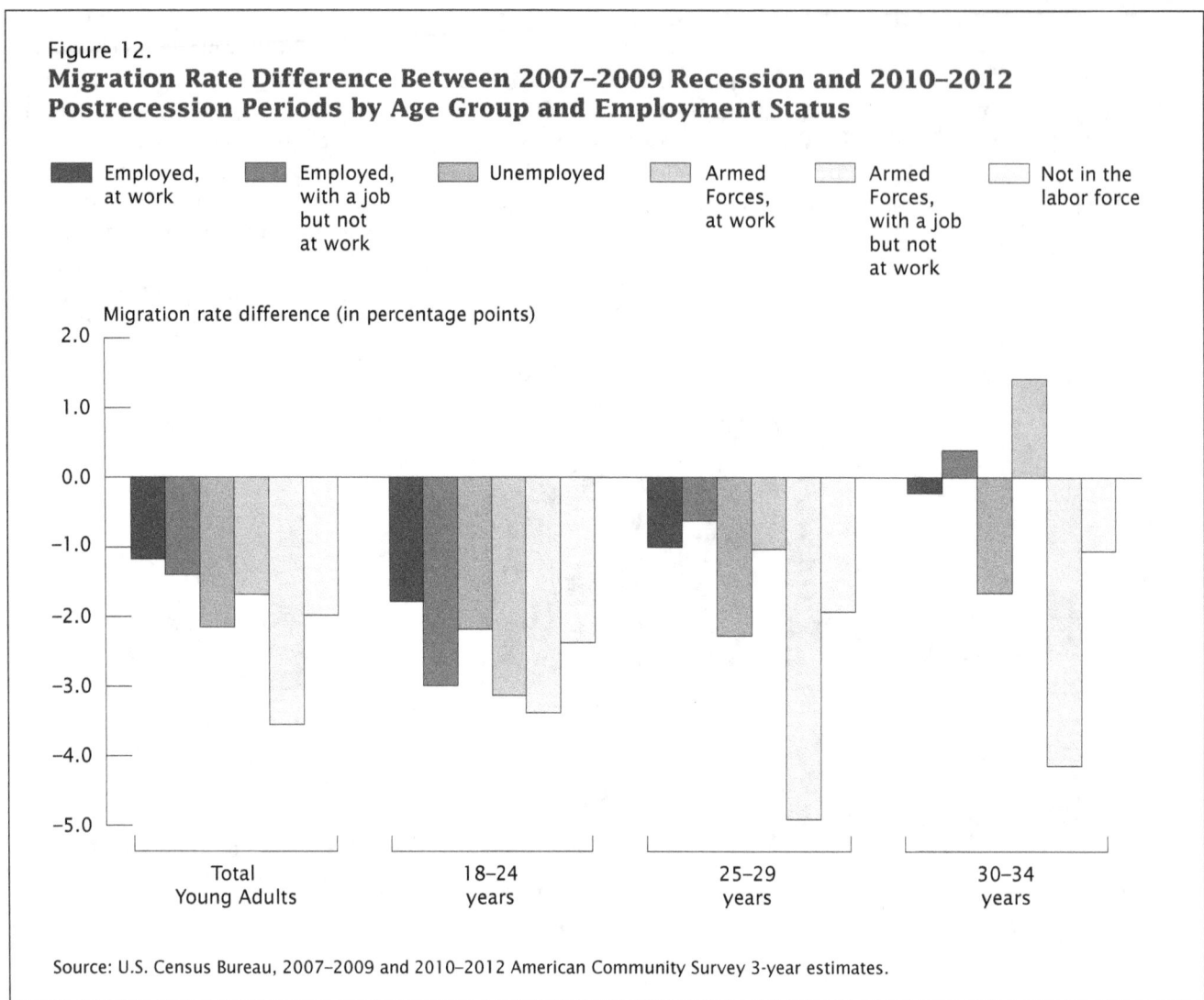

Figure 12.
Migration Rate Difference Between 2007–2009 Recession and 2010–2012 Postrecession Periods by Age Group and Employment Status

Employed, at work | Employed, with a job but not at work | Unemployed | Armed Forces, at work | Armed Forces, with a job but not at work | Not in the labor force

Migration rate difference (in percentage points)

Source: U.S. Census Bureau, 2007–2009 and 2010–2012 American Community Survey 3-year estimates.

GEOGRAPHIC MOVING PATTERNS OF YOUNG ADULTS

Consistently, young adults are the largest group of movers. The previous section showed differences in demographic characteristics of the three subgroups: 18- to 24-year-olds, 25- to 29-year-olds, and 30- to 34-year-olds. This section explores the geographic differences in migration for metropolitan areas with populations greater than or equal to 100,000 people, by examining the percentage of young adult inmovers.

INMOVERS

As mentioned earlier, the ACS asks respondents to identify where their place of residence was 1 year earlier. A mover is a person whose previous residence was different 1 year ago. While the previous section focused on all movers, this section focuses on inmovers.

INMOVER

A person was designated an inmover in this report if the individual's previous residence was in a different metro, micro, or nonmetropolitan area than her current residence, and her current residence was a metropolitan area with a total population of at least 100,000.

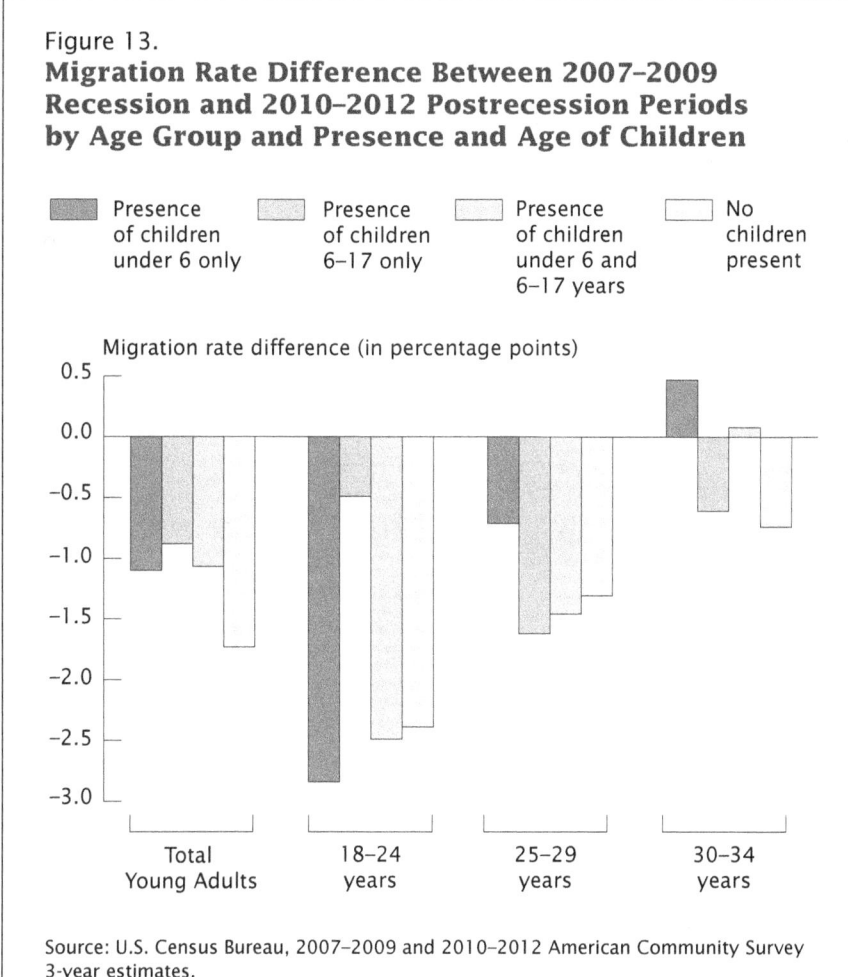

Figure 13.
Migration Rate Difference Between 2007–2009 Recession and 2010–2012 Postrecession Periods by Age Group and Presence and Age of Children

Legend:
- Presence of children under 6 only
- Presence of children 6–17 only
- Presence of children under 6 and 6–17 years
- No children present

Migration rate difference (in percentage points)

Categories: Total Young Adults, 18–24 years, 25–29 years, 30–34 years

Source: U.S. Census Bureau, 2007–2009 and 2010–2012 American Community Survey 3-year estimates.

An inmover was defined as an individual who lived in a metro area with a total population of at least 100,000 who did not live in the same metropolitan area in the previous year. An inmover's previous residence can be another metro, micro, or nonmetro area.

In the 2007–2009 recession period, there were 5,792,598 Total Young Adult inmovers to metros with a total population greater than 100,000, while in the 2010–2012 postrecession period there were only 5,626,816 (Table 4).

PERCENTAGE OF YOUNG ADULT INMOVERS

While it is important to note that large metropolitan areas gain the largest number of young adult movers, analyzing a metro's share of young adults moving into the area is another way to examine the migration of young adults. In order to determine which metropolitan areas acquired a larger share of young adult inmovers, the percentage of young adult inmovers of the total inmovers was calculated for each metro where the metro's

total population was greater than or equal to 100,000. Additionally, the metropolitan areas were divided into three groups based on the total population of the metro area—Group 1, small metros: 100,000 to 499,999; Group 2, medium metros: 500,000 to 999,999; and Group 3, large metros: 1,000,000 or greater.[27]

One key observation was that the 18- to 24-year-old group consistently had a higher percentage of inmovers when compared with the other two age groups, 25- to 29-year-olds and 30- to 34-year-olds. Table 5 notes metropolitan areas with total populations greater than 100,000 that were among the largest and smallest percentages of inmovers organized by metropolitan total population size and age group.

Figure 14 shows the percentage of young adult inmovers in relation to the total inmovers for the United States in the 2007–2009 recession period. Figure 15 shows the percentage of young adult inmovers in relation to the total inmovers for the United States in the 2010–2012 postrecession period. Gray colored metros had no statistical difference from the respective periods' national average. In the two periods, many metros in the Southwest and Florida were below the national average of the share of total young inmovers, while many metros in the Northeast were above the national average.

[27] Full tables for metro areas greater than 100,000 people is available at <http://www.census.gov/hhes/migration/files/acs/acs2007-2009/YAM_detailed-tables.xlsx>.

Table 4.
Inmovers to Metros (With a Population Greater Than 100,000) by Period

Inmovers	2007–2009 Recession period	Margin of error	2010–2012 Postrecession period	Margin of error
Total inmovers	11,747,283	52,480	11,414,533	47,616
Total Young Adult inmovers	5,792,598	30,490	5,626,816	23,734
Total Young Adult inmovers rate (percent)	49.3	0.2	49.3	0.2

Source: U.S. Census Bureau, 2007–2009 and 2010–2012 American Community Survey 3-year estimates.

LARGE METROS—POPULATION 1,000,000 OR GREATER

Recession

Among large metros (Table 5), Boston, MA; Rochester, NY; and Buffalo, NY, had the greatest percentage of Total Young Adult inmovers, above 50 percent. Among metros with the greatest percentage of 18- to 24-year-olds were Rochester, NY; Providence, RI; and Buffalo, NY. Salt Lake City, UT; San Jose, CA; and Denver, CO, were among the largest metros with the highest inmover percentage of 25- to 29-year-olds. Birmingham, AL; San Francisco, CA; and Austin, TX, were among large metros with the greatest percentage of inmovers aged 30 to 34. For these metros, about one person of every ten who moved into the metro was 30- to 34-years-old.

Postrecession

Among large metros, Providence, RI; Rochester, NY; and Boston, MA, had the greatest percentage of Total Young Adult inmovers, about 60 percent. Providence, RI; Rochester, NY; and Buffalo, NY, were still among large metros with the greatest 18- to 24-year-olds in the 2010–2012 postrecession period.[28] About 20 percent of all inmovers were aged 25 to 29 in San Jose, CA; Chicago, IL; and New York, NY. San Jose, CA; San Francisco, CA; and

Louisville, KY, were among large metros with the greatest percentage of 30- to 34-year-olds.

MEDIUM-SIZED METROS—POPULATION 500,000 TO 999,999

Recession

Among medium metros, Provo, UT; Madison, WI; and Toledo, OH, had the greatest percentage of Total Young Adult inmovers, which were between 60.3 and 65.3 percent. Provo, UT; Toledo, OH; and Springfield, MA, were among the top medium-sized metros with the greatest percentage of 18- to 24-year-olds. These metros ranged from 42.5 to 51.7 percent of their inmovers in this age group. Ogden, UT; Bakersfield, CA; and Omaha, NE, were among metros with the highest percentage of inmovers in the 25- to 29-year-old group. Each of these metros had about 17 percent of inmovers in this age group. Finally, New Haven, CT; Bridgeport, CT; and Worcester, MA, are among the medium-sized metros with the highest percentage of inmovers in the 30- to 34-year-old age group. However, these three metros had just over 10 percent of their inmovers in this age grouping.

Postrecession

In the 2010–2012 postrecession period, Madison, WI; Provo, UT; and Syracuse, NY, were among metros with the greatest percentage of Total Young Adult inmovers (about

65 percent, 64 percent, and 63 percent, respectively). Syracuse, NY; Provo, UT; and Springfield, MA, were among metros with the highest percentage of 18- to 24-year-olds. Each of these three metros have large universities or colleges located in the metro region. Ogden, UT; Honolulu, HI; and Durham-Chapel Hill, NC, were among medium metros with high percentages of 25- to 29-year-olds. Poughkeepsie, NY; Bakersfield, CA; and Bridgeport, CT, were among metros with the highest percentage of 30- to 34-year-olds.

SMALL METROPOLITAN AREAS—POPULATION 100,000 TO 499,999

Recession

In the 2007–2009 recession period, State College, PA; Ithaca, NY; and Blacksburg, VA, were among metros with the greatest percentage of Total Young Adult inmovers, about 76.7 to 78.0 percent. Blacksburg, VA; State College, PA; and Morgantown, WV, were among small metros with the highest percentages of 18- to 24-year-old inmovers. Coeur d'Alene, ID; Glens Falls, NY; and Odessa, TX, were among small metros with the highest percentages of 25- to 29-year-old inmovers. Laredo, TX; Madera, CA; and Monroe, LA, were among small metros with the greatest percentages of 30- to 34-year-olds.

---

[28] There was no statistical difference among the metros or between the periods.

Table 5.

Percentage of Young Adult Inmovers of All Inmovers by Age Group, Metropolitan Size, and Period—Con.

2007–2009 Recession Period Estimates			2010–2012 Postrecession Period Estimates		
Metropolitan area	Percent	Margin of error	Metropolitan area	Percent	Margin of error
TOTAL YOUNG ADULTS					
Large Metro Areas					
Among the largest					
Boston-Cambridge-Quincy, MA-NH Metro Area	58.1	1.6	Providence-New Bedford-Fall River, RI-MA Metro Area	60.5	2.7
Rochester, NY Metro Area	57.6	2.5	Rochester, NY Metro Area	59.7	2.7
Buffalo-Niagara Falls, NY Metro Area	57.1	3.1	Boston-Cambridge-Quincy, MA-NH Metro Area	59.2	1.3
Among the smallest					
Las Vegas-Paradise, NV Metro Area	37.7	1.4	Tampa-St. Petersburg-Clearwater, FL Metro Area	36.1	1.6
Miami-Fort Lauderdale-Pompano Beach, FL Metro Area	37.6	1.2	Las Vegas-Paradise, NV Metro Area	35.9	1.9
Tampa-St. Petersburg-Clearwater, FL Metro Area	36.4	1.3	Miami-Fort Lauderdale-Pompano Beach, FL Metro Area	35.8	1.4
Medium Metro Areas					
Among the largest					
Provo-Orem, UT Metro Area	65.3	3.1	Madison, WI Metro Area	65.1	2.5
Madison, WI Metro Area	62.1	2.9	Provo-Orem, UT Metro Area	64.0	2.7
Toledo, OH Metro Area	60.3	3.8	Syracuse, NY Metro Area	63.3	2.9
Among the smallest					
Lakeland-Winter Haven, FL Metro Area	35.8	2.7	Lakeland-Winter Haven, FL Metro Area	30.5	2.6
North Port-Bradenton-Sarasota, FL Metro Area	30.3	3.2	Cape Coral-Fort Myers, FL Metro Area	26.2	2.2
Cape Coral-Fort Myers, FL Metro Area	28.6	2.6	North Port-Bradenton-Sarasota, FL Metro Area	24.1	2.1
Small Metro Areas					
Among the largest					
State College, PA Metro Area	78.0	3.1	State College, PA Metro Area	84.2	2.8
Ithaca, NY Metro Area	77.2	4.2	Bloomington, IN Metro Area	77.8	3.5
Blacksburg-Christiansburg-Radford, VA Metro Area	76.7	3.4	Blacksburg-Christiansburg-Radford, VA Metro Area	77.5	4.2
Among the smallest					
Prescott, AZ Metro Area	28.4	4.2	Naples-Marco Island, FL Metro Area	25.5	4.3
Punta Gorda, FL Metro Area	25.0	5.3	Sebastian-Vero Beach, FL Metro Area	23.3	6.1
Sebastian-Vero Beach, FL Metro Area	24.0	4.8	Punta Gorda, FL Metro Area	22.4	4.5

See footnotes at end of table.

Table 5.
Percentage of Young Adult Inmovers of All Inmovers by Age Group, Metropolitan Size, and Period—Con.

2007–2009 Recession Period Estimates			2010–2012 Postrecession Period Estimates		
Metropolitan area	Percent	Margin of error	Metropolitan area	Percent	Margin of error
AGED 18–24					
Large Metro Areas					
Among the largest					
Rochester, NY Metro Area	37.2	3.3	Providence-New Bedford-Fall River, RI-MA Metro Area	37.2	2.8
Providence-New Bedford-Fall River, RI-MA Metro Area	33.9	3.2	Rochester, NY Metro Area	36.9	2.9
Buffalo-Niagara Falls, NY Metro Area	33.4	3.4	Buffalo-Niagara Falls, NY Metro Area	36.4	3.3
Among the smallest					
Las Vegas-Paradise, NV Metro Area	16.1	1.3	San Juan-Caguas-Guaynabo, PR Metro Area	16.1	2.3
Miami-Fort Lauderdale-Pompano Beach, FL Metro Area	15.5	1.0	Miami-Fort Lauderdale-Pompano Beach, FL Metro Area	15.5	1.0
Tampa-St. Petersburg-Clearwater, FL Metro Area.	14.5	1.1	Las Vegas-Paradise, NV Metro Area.	14.7	1.1
Medium Metro Areas					
Among the largest					
Provo-Orem, UT Metro Area	51.7	3.6	Syracuse, NY Metro Area	46.1	3.0
Toledo, OH Metro Area	43.8	4.0	Provo-Orem, UT Metro Area	46.0	3.1
Springfield, MA Metro Area	42.5	3.5	Springfield, MA Metro Area	43.1	4.3
Among the smallest					
Lakeland-Winter Haven, FL Metro Area	15.0	2.6	Lakeland-Winter Haven, FL Metro Area	12.0	2.1
North Port-Bradenton-Sarasota, FL Metro Area	13.0	2.0	Cape Coral-Fort Myers, FL Metro Area	11.6	1.5
Cape Coral-Fort Myers, FL Metro Area	11.2	2.0	North Port-Bradenton-Sarasota, FL Metro Area	9.4	1.3
Small Metro Areas					
Among the largest					
Blacksburg-Christiansburg-Radford, VA Metro Area	67.7	4.1	State College, PA Metro Area	75.4	3.2
State College, PA Metro Area	67.1	3.5	Blacksburg-Christiansburg-Radford, VA Metro Area	64.9	5.5
Morgantown, WV Metro Area	65.6	4.6	Bloomington, IN Metro Area	63.7	3.8
Among the smallest					
Punta Gorda, FL Metro Area	10.8	3.8	Ocala, FL Metro Area	9.6	2.6
Pascagoula, MS Metro Area	10.6	3.5	Port St. Lucie, FL Metro Area	8.6	1.5
Aguadilla-Isabela-San Sebastián, PR Metro Area.	10.3	4.0	Punta Gorda, FL Metro Area.	8.5	2.2

See footnotes at end of table.

Table 5.

Percentage of Young Adult Inmovers of All Inmovers by Age Group, Metropolitan Size, and Period—Con.

2007–2009 Recession Period Estimates			2010–2012 Postrecession Period Estimates		
Metropolitan area	Percent	Margin of error	Metropolitan area	Percent	Margin of error
AGED 25–29					
Large Metro Areas					
Among the largest					
Salt Lake City, UT Metro Area	18.8	1.6	San Jose-Sunnyvale-Santa Clara, CA Metro Area	18.2	1.3
San Jose-Sunnyvale-Santa Clara, CA Metro Area	18.4	1.6	Chicago-Joliet-Naperville, IL-IN-WI Metro Area	17.7	0.9
Denver-Aurora-Broomfield, CO Metro Area	18.4	1.1	New York-Northern New Jersey-Long Island, NY-NJ-PA Metro Area	17.6	0.6
Among the smallest					
Tucson, AZ Metro Area	12.3	1.6	Phoenix-Mesa-Glendale, AZ Metro Area	11.3	0.7
Jacksonville, FL Metro Area	12.2	1.2	Tampa-St. Petersburg-Clearwater, FL Metro Area	10.4	0.9
Providence-New Bedford-Fall River, RI-MA Metro Area	11.5	1.6	San Juan-Caguas-Guaynabo, PR Metro Area	10.1	1.9
Medium Metro Areas					
Among the largest					
Ogden-Clearfield, UT Metro Area	17.1	1.9	Ogden-Clearfield, UT Metro Area	17.8	1.9
Bakersfield, CA Metro Area	16.9	1.5	Honolulu, HI Metro Area	16.5	1.2
Omaha-Council Bluffs, NE-IA Metro Area	16.7	1.8	Durham-Chapel Hill, NC Metro Area	16.1	1.7
Among the smallest					
Provo-Orem, UT Metro Area	9.4	1.3	Greensboro-High Point, NC Metro Area	9.4	1.6
Greenville-Mauldin-Easley, SC Metro Area	9.1	1.3	North Port-Bradenton-Sarasota, FL Metro Area	8.9	1.6
Knoxville, TN Metro Area	8.5	1.4	Cape Coral-Fort Myers, FL Metro Area	8.1	1.7
Small Metro Areas					
Among the largest					
Coeur d'Alene, ID Metro Area	20.8	4.5	Appleton, WI Metro Area	20.8	4.0
Glens Falls, NY Metro Area	20.6	4.2	Monroe, MI Metro Area	17.7	4.0
Odessa, TX Metro Area	19.5	4.1	Fayetteville, NC Metro Area	17.5	1.6
Among the smallest					
Waco, TX Metro Area	5.2	1.6	Steubenville-Weirton, OH-WV Metro Area	5.8	3.1
Blacksburg-Christiansburg-Radford, VA Metro Area	4.6	1.3	Lima, OH Metro Area	5.6	2.4
Muncie, IN Metro Area	4.4	1.8	State College, PA Metro Area	4.8	1.4

See footnotes at end of table.

Table 5.
Percentage of Young Adult Inmovers of All Inmovers by Age Group, Metropolitan Size, and Period—Con.

2007–2009 Recession Period Estimates			2010–2012 Postrecession Period Estimates		
Metropolitan area	Percent	Margin of error	Metropolitan area	Percent	Margin of error
AGED 30–34					
Large Metro Areas					
Among the largest					
Birmingham-Hoover, AL Metro Area	12.5	1.5	San Jose-Sunnyvale-Santa Clara, CA Metro Area	13.3	1.1
San Francisco-Oakland-Fremont, CA Metro Area	12.2	0.7	San Francisco-Oakland-Fremont, CA Metro Area	12.7	0.8
Austin-Round Rock, TX Metro Area	12.0	1.1	Louisville/Jefferson County, KY-IN Metro Area	11.7	1.6
Among the smallest					
Rochester, NY Metro Area	7.6	1.2	Buffalo-Niagara Falls, NY Metro Area	8.0	1.6
Hartford-West Hartford-East Hartford, CT Metro Area	7.5	1.2	Sacramento–Arden-Arcade–Roseville, CA Metro Area	7.9	0.9
Providence-New Bedford-Fall River, RI-MA Metro Area	6.9	1.3	Orlando-Kissimmee-Sanford, FL Metro Area	7.6	0.9
Medium Metro Areas					
Among the largest					
New Haven-Milford, CT Metro Area	11.6	1.7	Poughkeepsie-Newburgh-Middletown, NY Metro Area	13.2	1.7
Bridgeport-Stamford-Norwalk, CT Metro Area	11.4	2.0	Bakersfield-Delano, CA Metro Area	12.2	1.5
Worcester, MA Metro Area	11.1	1.7	Bridgeport-Stamford-Norwalk, CT Metro Area	12.0	1.8
Among the smallest					
Toledo, OH Metro Area	5.6	1.3	Cape Coral-Fort Myers, FL Metro Area	6.6	1.6
Springfield, MA Metro Area	5.4	1.3	Springfield, MA Metro Area	6.1	1.3
Provo-Orem, UT Metro Area	4.1	0.8	North Port-Bradenton-Sarasota, FL Metro Area	5.8	1.0
Small Metro Areas					
Among the largest					
Laredo, TX Metro Area	15.7	4.8	Dalton, GA Metro Area	16.0	6.0
Madera-Chowchilla, CA Metro Area	15.0	3.1	Vineland-Millville-Bridgeton, NJ Metro Area	15.8	3.2
Monroe, LA Metro Area	13.6	4.2	El Centro, CA Metro Area	15.5	3.4
Among the smallest					
Gainesville, FL Metro Area	3.1	0.9	Terre Haute, IN Metro Area	3.5	1.3
Lafayette, IN Metro Area	3.1	0.9	St. Cloud, MN Metro Area	3.4	1.3
Altoona, PA Metro Area	2.9	1.7	Bowling Green, KY Metro Area	2.5	1.3

Note: An inmover is anyone who moved from one metropolitan, micropolitan, or nonmetropolitan area to a different metropolitan area. Recession and postrecession periods use the 2010–2012 CBSA metropolitan names. Durham-Chapel Hill, NC, was categorized as a small-sized metro in the 2007–2009 recession period and a medium-sized metro in the 2010–2012 postrecession period.
Source: U.S. Census Bureau, 2007–2009 and 2010–2012 American Community Survey 3-year estimates.

Postrecession

In the 2010–2012 postrecession period, State College, PA; Bloomington, IN; and Blacksburg, VA, were among small metros with the largest percentage, about three-quarters, of Total Young Adult inmovers. State College, PA; Blacksburg, VA; and Bloomington, IN, were among small metros with shares of 18- to 24-year-old inmovers between 63.7 and 75.4 percent. In fact, among the top small metros with the greatest percentage of 18- to 24-year-olds were locations with large colleges or universities. Appleton, WI; Monroe, MI; and Fayetteville, NC, were among the top small metros with the largest percentage of 25- to 29-year-olds. Dalton, GA; Vineland, NJ; and El Centro, CA, were among the largest percentage of inmovers for small metro areas.

SUMMARY

Overall, migration for the Total Young Adult group decreased between the two periods. In examining the three subgroups—small, medium, and large metros—patterns of migration emerged. First, for the 18- to 24-year-old group, metro areas with a college or university appeared to be a magnet for this group. In fact, regardless of the size of the metropolitan area, metros with institutions of higher education had a large proportion of inmovers. As presented in the demographic section, 18- to 24-year-olds were the age group that was most likely to move. This age group was also a large share of inmovers. Second, for the 25- to 29-year-old age group, the total share of inmovers was lower than that of 18- to 24-year-olds, but higher than those aged 30-34. Additionally, the 25- to 29-year-old group appeared to have a higher percentage of inmovers to metros with a military presence, for example Ogden-Clearfield, UT, and Honolulu, HI. This corroborated previous findings that people in the military service were frequent movers.[29] The importance of metropolitan area characteristics, location for universities or colleges, a military facility, or employment opportunities, are important to understanding the migration of young adults.

CONCLUSION

Young adults have historically been drivers of migration and continue to move in great numbers as recent data showed. This report has presented differences in young adults' migration rates when considering demographic, socioeconomic, and family characteristics, as well as the places young adults moved. Furthermore, differing migration rates across these characteristics were compounded when looking over time, as most young adult groups saw decreased migration between the recession and postrecession periods. In examining the metro size and its share of young adults who are inmovers to the metro, some small metros had greater shares when compared to larger metropolitan places.

SOURCE OF THE ESTIMATES

The American Community Survey (ACS) is a nationwide survey designed to provide communities with reliable and timely demographics, social, economic, and housing data for congressional districts, counties, places, and other localities every year. It has an annual sample size of about 3.5 million addresses across the United States and Puerto Rico and includes both housing units and group quarters (e.g., nursing homes and prisons). The ACS is conducted in every county throughout the nation, and every municipio in Puerto Rico, where it is called the Puerto Rico Community Survey. Beginning in 2006, ACS data for 2005 were released for geographic areas with populations of 65,000 and greater. For information on the ACS sample design and other topics, visit <www.census.gov/acs/www>.

---

[29] Melanie A. Rapino and Julia Beckhusen, "The Migration of Military Spouses using the 2007–2011 5-Year American Community Survey," Working Paper No. 2013-25, U.S. Census Bureau, Washington, DC, 2012.

Figure 14.
Percent Young Adult Inmovers by Metropolitan Statistical Area: 2007–2009

(Data based on sample. For information on confidentiality protection, sampling error, nonsampling error, and definitions, see *www.census.gov/acs/www/*)

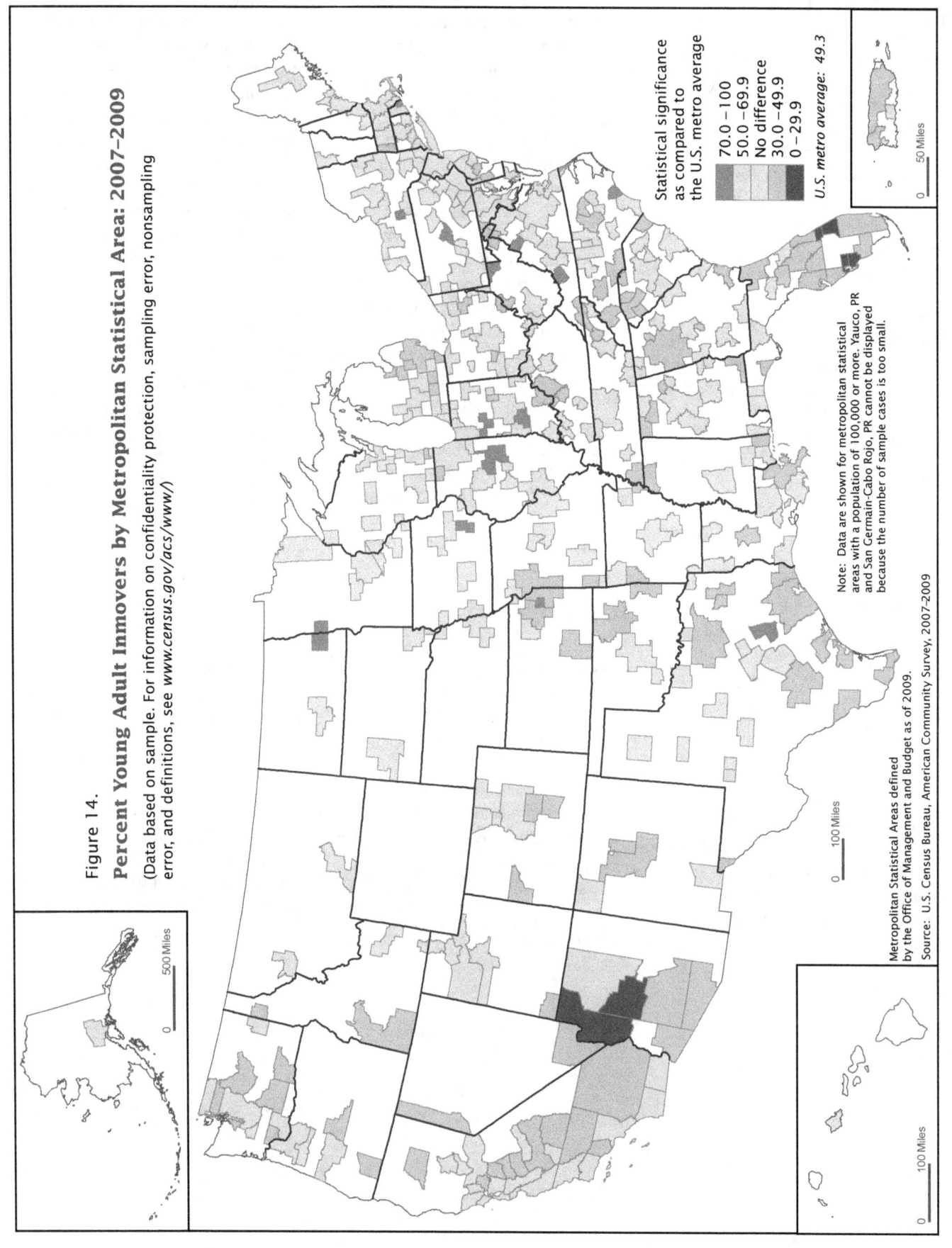

Statistical significance as compared to the U.S. metro average

- 70.0 – 100
- 50.0 – 69.9
- No difference
- 30.0 – 49.9
- 0 – 29.9

U.S. metro average: 49.3

Note: Data are shown for metropolitan statistical areas with a population of 100,000 or more. Yauco, PR and San Germain-Cabo Rojo, PR cannot be displayed because the number of sample cases is too small.

Metropolitan Statistical Areas defined by the Office of Management and Budget as of 2009.

Source: U.S. Census Bureau, American Community Survey, 2007–2009.

0   100 Miles

0   500 Miles

0   100 Miles

0   50 Miles

Figure 15.

Percent Young Adult Inmovers by Metropolitan Statistical Area: 2010–2012

(Data based on sample. For information on confidentiality protection, sampling error, nonsampling error, and definitions, see *www.census.gov/acs/www/*)

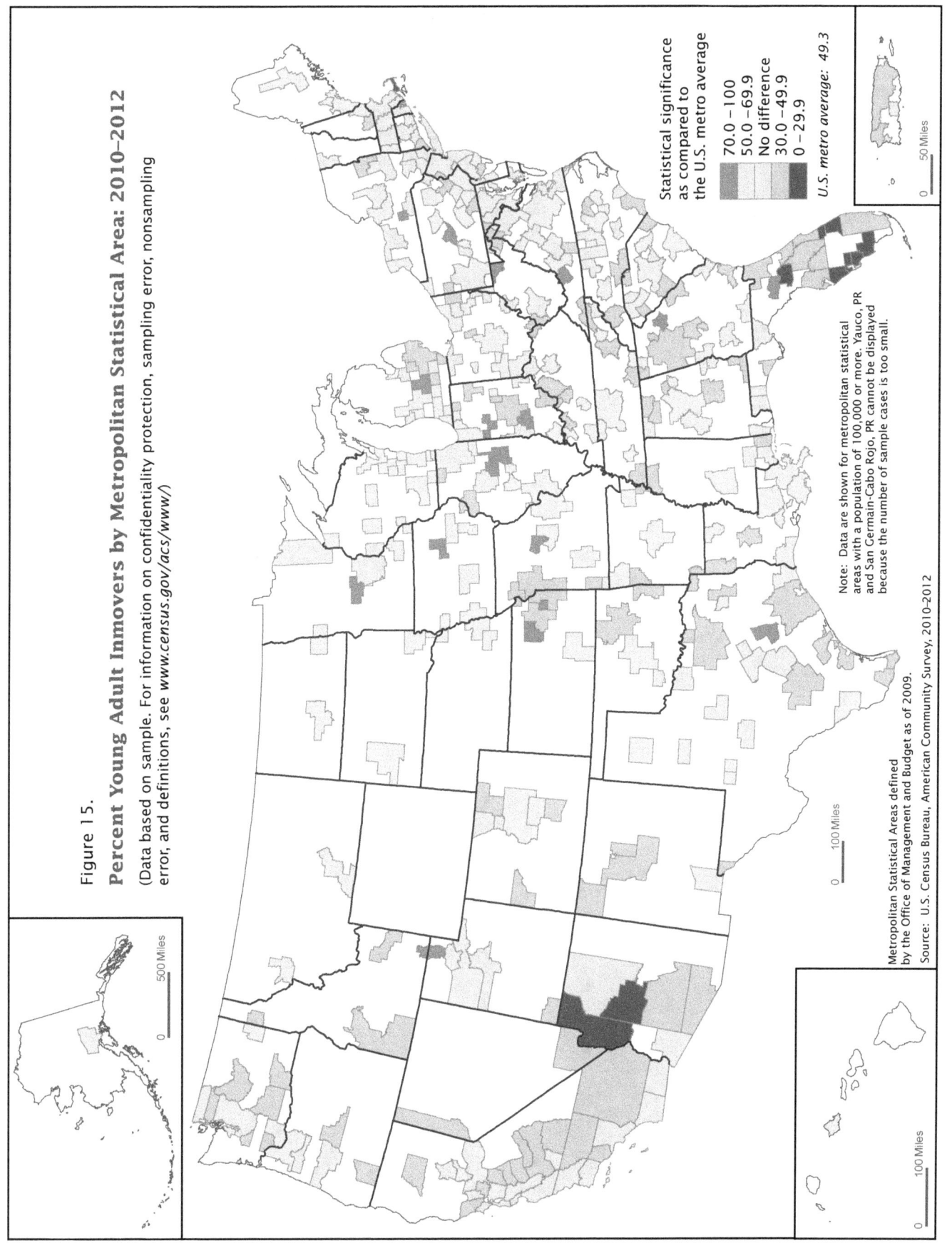

Statistical significance
as compared to
the U.S. metro average

70.0 – 100
50.0 – 69.9
No difference
30.0 – 49.9
0 – 29.9

U.S. metro average: 49.3

50 Miles

Note: Data are shown for metropolitan statistical areas with a population of 100,000 or more. Yauco, PR and San Germain-Cabo Rojo, PR cannot be displayed because the number of sample cases is too small.

Metropolitan Statistical Areas defined by the Office of Management and Budget as of 2009.

Source: U.S. Census Bureau, American Community Survey, 2010–2012.

100 Miles

500 Miles

100 Miles

ACCURACY OF THE ESTIMATES

The data presented in this report are based on the ACS sample interviewed between 2007 and 2009 and between 2010 and 2012. The estimates based on this sample approximate the actual values and represent the entire United States and Puerto Rico resident household and group quarters population. Sampling error is the difference between an estimate based on a sample and the corresponding value that would be obtained if the estimate were based on the entire population (as from a census). Measures of the sampling error are provided in the form of margins of error for all estimates included in this report. All comparative statements in this report have undergone statistical testing, and comparisons are significant at the 90 percent level unless otherwise noted. In addition to sampling error, nonsampling error may be introduced during any of the operations used to collect and process survey data such as editing, reviewing, or keying data from questionnaires. For more information on sampling and estimation methods, confidentiality protection, and sampling and nonsampling errors, please see the ACS Accuracy of the Data document located at <www.census.gov /acs/www/data_documentation /documentation main>.

For more information on domestic migration, go to the U.S. Census Bureau's Web site at <www.census .gov/topics/population/migration .html>, or contact the Journey to Work and Migration Statistics Branch at 301-763-2454 or <sehsd.migration@census.gov>.

SUGGESTED CITATION

Benetsky, Megan J., Charlynn Burd, and Melanie Rapino, "Young Adult Migration: 2007–2009 to 2010–2012," *American Community Survey Reports*, ACS-31, U.S. Census Bureau, Washington, DC, 2015.